k2.

D1436948

COUNTRY CRAFTS TODAY

COUNTRY CRAFTS
TODAY

J. E. MANNERS

DAVID & CHARLES

NEWTON ABBOT   LONDON   VANCOUVER

Set in 11pt on 13pt Garamond and printed in
Great Britain by Biddles Limited Guildford for
David & Charles (Holdings) Limited
South Devon House Newton Abbot Devon

Published in Canada by Douglas David & Charles
Limited 3645 McKechnie Drive
West Vancouver BC

CONTENTS

LIST OF ILLUSTRATIONS

INTRODUCTION

COUNTRY CRAFTS are those that are practised in a rural community by men of skill, patience, dexterity and experience. This book is an attempt to record them, before some vanish completely. All the photographs have been taken during the last six years and many of the craftsmen portrayed are of a ripe old age with nobody to follow in their footsteps.

Most rural crafts thrived in the past. Apart from places either near the sea or on navigable rivers, the villages were served by bad roads which were rough in summer and wellnigh impassable in winter. Packhorses moving along the packways and ridgeways keeping to the higher grounds brought necessary supplies such as salt and metal tools, unobtainable locally, but to a large extent communities had to cater for their own needs, and over the years supply and demand became evenly balanced.

The improvements in roads did not start until the coming of the turnpikes from about 1760 onwards. Soon after this, the construction of canals began on an increasing scale, with an extensive network being built up, which brought cheap coal to a large number of districts. Finally, from 1830 onwards, came the railways. Each development had an adverse effect on local crafts though most of them survived until this century, during the course of which they have been very severely reduced. Coupled with better communications came the competition of mass-produced factory articles, generally cheaper but less good. Finally, the arrival of the internal combustion engine tractors, which replaced horses, put most farriers, wheelwrights and blacksmiths out of business.

To the country craftsman life was always a struggle for existence. In rural areas the work tended to be seasonal, more jobs being available in the summer, particularly during harvest. A number of the men found winter employment in the coppices cutting wood, making hurdles and faggots, and felling trees. The more fortunate, like blacksmiths, farriers and wheelwrights, had less difficulty in coping with seasonal fluctuations.

Prices were stable and it was almost impossible to raise them, so that few were ever able to become rich. This was particularly true of those dealing with farmers who are, by tradition, dilatory payers, suffering as they do from periodic depressions.

Most of the crafts were passed down from father to son, probably only the eldest, and thus the secrets were kept in the family, preventing outsiders from setting up business in opposition. Apprenticeships took a long time, anything up to seven years, so no trade could expand quickly. Should a craftsmen take on an apprentice the latter had to pay for the privilege. Nowadays an apprentice wants a good wage to start with, although in many trades he is unable to earn his keep for a long time. Furthermore, during the learning period the craftsmen is slowed down while he instructs his pupil. There is a suggestion that the government might make a grant to apprentices to supplement their wages during the early training period and some government-sponsored courses are now available. These, however, are mostly to improve the standards of young craftsmen.

A sad fact is that so many craftsmen are bad businessmen. On the whole, their average age is high, many left school very early and they do not understand inflation.

Craftsmen are primarily concerned with having the necessities of life rather than the luxuries. The indelible memory of the depression years when wages were calculated to a halfpenny has made the older men extremely cautious. Their children are different. There is a reluctance to follow in the steps of their fathers when they see how much easier it is to make money in a factory or by working on a building site. Nor do the fathers press their sons to follow them. They have seen bad times, worked long hours, as do most self-employed people, and do not want their sons to have such a hard time.

They tend to be nature's gentlemen. In a small community they have to be obliging to all their customers, they are slow and rhythmical in their movements, their muscles are kept in good trim, they dare not lose time due to illness, they keep an even temper, drown any sorrows in beer (though unable to afford the quantity consumed by their forebears) and have disciplined themselves to be contented and philosophical in their outlook.

Future employment in some essential crafts is assured for the reduced numbers at work. In this category are thatchers, farriers and saddlers. Others doing well in luxury or non-essential crafts are wrought-iron workers, potters and hand brickmakers. Their products are in steady demand amongst the discerning and those that want a more individual type of article.

Dwindling crafts include coopering, making footwear by hand, hedge laying, basketry and hurdle making, though it is unlikely that any of these will completely die out.

There are only a minimal number of workers left employed in some crafts—for instance slate quarrying. Today there are comparatively few horn workers, flint knappers, wheelwrights, millers and charcoal burners. But the numbers of certain craftsmen, such as cider, clay pipe, and cricket bat makers are increasing. Others have virtually vanished, amongst which are chair bodgers, rope makers, dew pond makers and treen (wooden utensils) workers. Such crafts as weaving and making corn dollies, however, have been revived as leisure pursuits, and some people make a living out of them.

The fact that an article is craftsman made does not necessarily mean it is good, as there are differing standards in all trades. The designs may be poor or unbalanced and the workmanship variable. The present-day craftsman has to produce a certain volume of output in order to make a living and as not all purchasers will pay for expensive refinements, it may well be that quantity rather than quality has to take precedence.

Parallel to the near-disappearance of a great many crafts, is a revival of interest in them, shown wherever demonstrations are given at events like agricultural shows.

In spite of their difficulties as a whole, the craftsmen belong to a minority who are proud of their work, set a high standard and are contented.

From time to time prices have been quoted in the text which are approximately those prevailing in 1974. With inflation these will quickly become out of date probably rising by 10 per cent a year, though in many cases, much more.

CHAPTER I

WOOD AND WOODLAND CRAFTS

WOOD

WOOD IS one of the most useful and widely used materials in the country. Until Elizabethan times there was an adequate supply, but the ensuing period of increased demand means that today we have to import the majority of our requirements. In Tudor times it was needed in quantity for building ships and houses, charcoal burning, brick and glassmaking etc. Up till then no forestry had been practised, animals were allowed to graze the young saplings and villagers could take all they could get by hook or by crook. Therefore there was no new growth and all this produced a timber shortage that has never been rectified. The native trees are nearly all hardwood with oak, ash, beech and elm predominating. Hardwoods are the trees that shed their leaves in winter. The name is somewhat misleading as some hardwoods such as poplar are in fact very soft, while some softwoods (which are largely pines) are comparatively hard.

Every year a tree makes a growth ring immediately under the bark, and by counting these when a tree has been sawn through, its age can be established. The outside inch or so, referred to as sap wood, is softer and immature and usually discarded for the harder heartwood.

In the spring and summer the sap rises, making the tree grow and produce leaves. In the past trees were never felled at this time, the forester waiting till winter when they were dormant. With modern kiln drying, however, felling now goes on all the year round.

A newly cut tree is referred to as being 'green' and in this condition it is best for cleaving with wedges or axes. Cleft wood splits down the grain and is stronger than a sawn piece which may have cuts through knots and across the grain.

Trees always used to be left to season slowly for a number of years and represented tied-up capital which woodworkers could ill afford. The object of seasoning is to let the sap dry out gradually so minimising the risk of the wood splitting and warping. Wood never dries out completely and timber 100 years old will shrink and expand with the humidity, as some people find out when they put central heating in an old house.

The majority of hardwood trees do not mature for well over 100 years—a deterrent to growing them as a commercial proposition, particularly as they prefer the best agricultural land. The vast majority of commercial plantations, probably about 99 per cent, are of conifers with sitka and Norwegian spruce predominating. Native trees in this category are the Scots pine and larch. An average age of a conifer, before it is felled, is sixty years, but valuable thinnings are cut at intervals before this.

There was a steady demand by craftsmen for bent wood so that they could avoid cutting across the grain as much as possible. This type of wood was necessary for ships' timbers, cruck-built houses, waggon shafts and much of the wheelwrights' work. Now all wood is wanted with straight grain free from the knots caused by large branches.

All trees deteriorate after reaching their prime with branches dying. The rotting can spread to the centre eventually making the trees valueless as timber and only fit for firewood.

Where there is a woodland composed of hardwood trees, underneath is frequently some coppiced wood. This mostly is made up of hazel, sweet chestnut, birch or ash that is cut to ground level at regular intervals for hurdles, fences, faggots and similar uses.

Another form of preservation sometimes encountered is pollarding, a practice whereby trees are cut off about 10 feet from the ground and allowed to sprout. Burnham beeches provide a good example of this. The wood was used for furnaces and cut off at intervals of about twenty-five years, with the result that the bole or trunk of the tree became excessively large round the girth. In towns where woodland trees are pollarded to stop too much growth, the results look regrettably far from handsome.

No longer do the few remaining craftsmen go out and select their own choice of trees to fell. They do not have the time for this so buy from a merchant. The unhappy likelihood is that the trees will be foreign-grown.

HEDGES AND HEDGE LAYING

Most of our hedges date from around the time of George III when parliamentary enclosure of the open hedgeless fields was rapidly gaining momentum. Most of the awards specifically stated that the boundaries had to be fenced within a year. Bearing in mind that an enclosure of 40 acres needed a mile of fence, the heavy demand for wood seriously depleted the woodlands in many places. The original fences consisted of hardwood posts and bars which would usually have been cleft. The internal fencing could be done at leisure. In most cases these wooden fences were replaced by hedges of blackthorn (sloe) and hawthorn (may), sometimes referred to as quickset, these plants being supplemented by elm. Seedlings had to be grown and planted in the hedges when ready some four years later. These hedges took about twenty years to mature and grow into a really effective barrier and it is not till the end of the eighteenth century that the craft of cutting and laying them is first mentioned. At the same time that the fields were enclosed drainage ditches were made and the excavated earth frequently formed the bed of the hedge.

When enclosures were made by Acts of Parliament, officials usually laid out straight roads between places. In country districts, however, one sometimes encounters well-hedged narrow roads that keep turning at right angles. These may well result from the original track following the perimeter of early voluntary enclosures.

The voluntary enclosure of land had been going on since medieval days so some hedges may be very old. Those making boundaries, often grown on the sides of the embanked boundary ditches, may well go back to Saxon times.

While planted hedges may have consisted only of thorn and elm in their early days, other trees later found their way into them, like oak, beech and ash in particular, along with other native kinds such as holly and hornbeam in lesser numbers and willows which so frequently take root and grow after having been driven in as stakes.

When a mature hedgerow tree is felled it can be of interest to count the growth rings and establish the age of the tree. This may give some indication of the date of the enclosing hedge though the tree may have grown up later.

Statistics about hedges are hard to come by and probably not very accurate, but it is probable that there are 600,000 miles of them in England today. They are continually being grubbed out at the rate of thousands of miles a year. The estimates vary widely, but about 7,000 miles annually is a possible figure and this has been kept up for the last twenty-five years.

The value of hedges is unquestioned. They give shelter to stock, act as windbreaks, mark boundaries, help to stop soil erosion and keep in the stock, in addition to providing valuable hardwood and supporting bird life.

Stock farmers tend to like hedges, while arable farmers want large fields for their big harvesting machinery. Many regard them as a nuisance rather than an asset in these days when everything is run with commercial requirements nearly always overriding other considerations. When fences are required it is easier nowadays to use barbed wire or an electric fence than hedges. Barbed wire is an American invention of a hundred years ago, while electric fencing came in and gathered momentum from the 1930s onwards.

A further hazard for hedges is the fire risk resulting in the modern practice of burning unwanted straw in the fields after harvest. Some of these fires get out of hand, scorching and sometimes killing hedges.

The cutting and laying of hedges has always been a winter job, usually carried out at the time when ditches are being remade. In former times there was a surplus of cheap agricultural labour and maintaining the hedges served the dual purpose of giving winter employment and keeping the estate in order—a job more easily done when the undergrowth is dead and the leaves have fallen.

Today labour costs are rising all the time, compelling many farmers to mechanise as far as possible with some unhappy-looking results when it comes to cutting and trimming hedges. Neatly cut and laid hedges that can be so pleasing to the eye are becoming fewer every year.

Luckily, there are still enough farmers left to keep alive the old and skilled craft, particularly in the Midlands, where competitions are still held. There is no better way of maintaining the standard.

The hedgelayer's equipment is comparatively modest. He needs little more than a bill hook, a long-handled slasher, possibly an axe, and a pair of strong leather gloves to protect against thorns.

Every individual has his own particular way of laying a hedge but all follow the same basic method. To restore order to an over-grown hedge the first operation is to clear away the undergrowth and then trim the sides to the required width. This is done by upward strokes of the slasher which avoid splintering the wood. All is then ready for laying the hedge. The unwanted wood such as elder and bramble is cut out. The usual practice is to start from the left and work towards the right preferably moving uphill. The stem of the first tree is cut with the bill hook within about a foot of the ground and bent over at an angle of 60° or more. The stem must not be cut right through, since enough of it must be left to allow the sap to rise for every plant in a good hedge is living.

About every 2 feet there should be a vertical post. This can be a living sapling that is cut off at the final height of the hedge, which is normally a little over 3 feet. In the absence of suitable saplings in the hedge, posts are driven in. They can be of any available wood, such as hazel, oak, ash and chestnut, either cleft or in the round. Their life is a comparatively short one as they are replaced when the hedge is relaid after a few years. The process of cutting and laying the saplings, which can finish up 10 feet long, continues throughout the length of the hedge.

The final operation is that of binding the top of the hedge, by entwining rods called heathers in and out of the vertical posts. Hazel or elm are very suitable for this, and so is briar, though used less frequently than in the past.

A carefully laid, completely stock-proof hedge with every plant living. The binding along the top keeps it rigid

Here and there a tree will be allowed to grow to maturity and a very large percentage of our hardwood is preserved in this way. If well spaced these trees have plenty of room to develop, act as windbreaks and give shelter to livestock. In many parts of the country elms predominate with their suckers frequently forming much of the hedge. Unluckily this tree is subject to Dutch elm disease and may lose some of its popularity. A good feature about the hedgerow elm is the fact that it has a tall compact growth with a small crown so that vegetation grows readily underneath. The leaves of a tree such as a beech prevent the penetration of sunlight and discourage growth below.

The layering of a well-laid and living hedge forces the branches to tiller out, particularly at the bottom, so making it stock-proof, which is usually the prime function.

A hedger might be able to cut and lay a chain each day or about 100 yards in a week. It is difficult to give exact figures because a long-neglected hedge takes far more time to lay than one that has been regularly maintained and trimmed. Knowing the agricultural wage, which rises every year with inflation, a farmer can easily assess the cost of his hedge laying and he might prefer to call in a professional to do the job. Unfortunately it is cheaper and quicker to run an electric fence to keep in the livestock or to use barbed wire, which regrettably is sometimes nailed to the hedgerow trees, eventually becoming embedded to ruin somebody's saw in years to come.

Mechanisation now competes everywhere with the craftsman. Hedges are frequently ruthlessly cut by circular saws mounted on tractors, which produce ugly hedges, all top and no bottom, and useless for keeping in stock quite apart from the effect it has in diminishing bird life.

More recently flail cutters are being used. These splinter and mutilate the ends of the branches, but are claimed to make the shoots break out lower down and perpetuate the density of the hedge. Since the cuttings are disintegrated and do not have to be gathered up afterwards, this method is likely to gain in popularity.

Economics frequently drive farmers into practices which they do not really like, and few besides the large and efficient can afford the luxury of a pleasing aesthetic look to their property in the form of well-laid hedges. Fortunately there are still a number who are still able and willing to continue cutting and laying their hedges in the traditional manner.

BESOM BROOMS

Besom brooms have been made for several centuries and there is still nothing to touch them for sweeping up in gardens. They are almost always made of birch brushwood, though very occasionally of heather, with a handle of any suitable wood that is available locally.

Of the declining number of men still making them, some cut the wood themselves, but others prefer to buy their materials.

The birchwood for the brooms is cut from the crowns of coppiced trees when they have attained an age of about eight years. With less coppice work being done it is not always easy to obtain the necessary supplies. The wood is cut in the winter when in the dormant stage, made into faggots, and then stacked in the open for a year to season with a covering of thatch or corrugated iron to keep out the elements.

Normally the besoms are made in the open though it is preferable to have a shed nearby so work can continue during bad weather.

To make the main part of the broom, first some brushwood is bent double to form a core. Around this is carefully placed the birch brushwood and the whole lot is bound together tightly with two bands of wire about 6 inches apart. Wire is now used almost universally as it is more convenient and quicker than the traditional binding of withy. Occasionally the bindings are of split cane, oak slivers or brambles but as valuable time is lost in the preparation of these they have lost favour and are not often seen.

To bind the broom the operator sits on a contraption called a horse with a chair seat fixed at one end of a frame whilst the other

A working-area for making besom brooms

has a foot-operated brake or clamp to hold either the wire when it is being pulled tight around the broom or the handle when being shaped and trimmed. After binding, the top of the broom is cut off square with an axe on a chopping log. The best handles have the bark removed and any roughness smoothed with a draw knife. The end is slightly pointed to help in the last operation of forcing it into the heart of the brush and then being banged down till it has gone in about 9 inches. Finally a nail is hammered in between the binding wire to keep the handle in position.

The craftsmen work with great speed and can turn out about eight dozen or ten dozen a day when everything is set up. Even so the supply cannot meet the demand.

Besoms are still comparatively cheap to buy in the shops with the craftsman himself receiving about half the shop selling price. The price depends on the size which is measured round the circumference at the top of the broom, the average being 12 inches.

23

HAY RAKES

The demand for hay rakes is now very small and few craftsmen are left in the trade. The details of their construction and the wood used varies regionally.

One old-fashioned craftsman makes his rakes as follows. The head which is the most important part is made out of cleft willow which has been left to season for a year. A round of wood is cut to a length of 28 inches and cleft into pieces with a cross section of $1\frac{1}{4}$ inches. These are trimmed and shaped with a draw knife following which thirteen holes are drilled through at regular intervals to take the teeth. The teeth are also of willow 6 inches in length and roughly cleft to shape. The final fashioning of them is done in a tool consisting of a tube of metal the size required for the teeth. This has a sharp cutting rim. The rough-shaped tooth is placed upon this rim and a sharp blow on top with a wooden mallet knocks it through the tube where it falls on to the ground below as a nicely shaped tooth with a circular cross section.

These teeth are hammered into the holes already bored in the rake head which is held in a vice during this operation. The teeth are then given points by using a draw knife. At the same time, care is taken to trim them all so they have the same length, as a protruding tooth will spoil the smooth working of the finished rake.

The handles are made from 6 foot poles of any available wood, with ash, alder, birch or willow predominating. If bent they are first straightened by steam. When a hay rake is being used, one hand holds it firm whilst the other slides up and down, so smoothness is essential. This is achieved using a circular plane which fits over the handle and is revolved round it to give the required finish. A cut of 2 feet in length is made in one end of the handle and a metal band fixed around the top of the cut to prevent further splitting. The ends of the split are opened out and trimmed with a draw

(Opposite) Smoothing the handle of a rake with a circular plane

knife to enable it to be fitted through two holes which are made in the rake head. These holes are 6 inches apart and very carefully angled so that the angle between the handle and head is coming in at 85°, held in position with nails.

The finished article, which takes $1\frac{1}{2}$ hours to make, is light, well balanced and easy to use, the design having stood up to the test of time.

There is another completely different method of making hay rakes, using as much mechanisation as possible. In this case, the rake is made entirely of ash which has to be comparatively free of knots, a quality that is not so easily obtainable. An ash log is first cut into pieces of $1\frac{1}{2}$ inches $\times$ $1\frac{1}{4}$ inches cross section, 33 inches in length, for a seventeen-toothed head. The edges of these pieces of wood are chamfered all round to give a neat, clean finish. They are then put in a jig and the seventeen holes are bored 2 inches apart and about $\frac{7}{16}$ inches in diameter.

The teeth are made by feeding a length of ash through a dowelling machine coming out with a $\frac{1}{2}$ inch cross section. These dowels are cut into 6-inch lengths and are hammered into the holes already in the rake head and, being of slightly larger diameter than the holes, make a good tight fit.

The head is then clamped down at the required angle and all the ends of the teeth are sawn off obliquely by a circular saw.

The handles are machine cut from a sizeable baulk of timber to a square cross section and then rounded in the dowelling machine subsequently being fitted to the head in the same way as described earlier in the chapter. By these methods about two dozen rakes can be assembled in an hour once the material has been cut.

The finished rakes look quite different. The first type made of cleft wood is lighter and has the maximum strength as there is no cutting across the grain. The latter has a more finished appearance but is somewhat heavier being of ash which is very straight grained if good quality wood can be obtained.

Both types of rake do a first-class job and there is no difficulty in selling as many as can be made.

HURDLES

WATTLE HURDLES

The main use for hurdles was for penning in sheep or making folds so that fields could be quartered off to enable the fodder to be rationed and the ground to become well trodden and manured at the same time. Rising labour costs coupled with the arrival of electric fencing has meant that hurdles are no longer the answer to present-day problems.

Before the advent of nitrogen fertilisers, the manuring of the ground by sheep was essential for growing cereal crops, so much so that in the feudal system it was obligatory for part of the time to fold them on the land of the lord of the manor. Satisfactory crops could not be grown without the aid of 'the golden hoof'.

One of the first tasks for the shepherd every morning was to set up the new fold for penning in the sheep when they returned from their pasture later in the day. This operation involved moving something like 100 hurdles. He would need about double this number altogether because the sheep had to be penned in one fold while the next was being made. The hurdles were invariably of woven hazel called wattle and a shepherd would carry four of these, 3 feet in height and 6 feet long, slung over his shoulder held by a stick which went through the twilly holes left specially for this purpose. The pointed-end poles that projected from the ends of the hurdle were pushed into the ground. A hole was first made with a metal bar if the earth was hard.

Hurdles were also put to a number of other uses such as making temporary gates, plugging gaps in hedges, and in market places, where they are still used quite extensively particularly at such places as Wilton sheep fair. When land enclosure was taking place they were very often set up to mark the boundaries while the newly planted hedges had time to grow. Today the main demand is mostly for garden screens or partitions in heights ranging from 3 feet to 6 feet.

The craft of making hurdles still lingers in some districts and demand is well in excess of supply. Most of the craftsmen still plying the trade are aged sixty or upwards. These men work the hazel coppices cutting the wood when it is around eight years of age. This cutting was formerly carried out during the winter months when the trees were dormant and there was little sap. This fitted in well with the yearly cycle as it provided winter work which was scarce and released the men in the summer months to help on the farms and bring in the harvest. Now the coppices are cut all the year round though the wood cut in summer will not last as long as that cut in the winter, a fact that escapes the notice of the dealers and the buying public. A hurdle should last seven to eight years under normal conditions. The trimmings of brushwood used to be made up into faggots or bavins used for firing bread ovens up till the war. They are now burnt as waste apart from a few kept for pea sticks.

Making a hurdle. Before being threaded back, the hazel rod is given a half twist to prevent the fibres from breaking

The work of cutting and preparing the wood takes about a third of a man's time. First a piece of slightly curved wood called a mould is laid on the ground and securely fixed. This has ten holes bored in it spaced at equidistant intervals into which are placed the vertical stakes called sails. The two end ones are slightly thicker than the others, ash sometimes being used for these if available. The sails are carefully cut to a length of around 4 feet to make a 3-feet high hurdle. Having set these up, a long, thin hazel rod is woven in and out of them and on reaching the end is given a half twist and threaded back. This twist is an essential part of the operation. If a piece of hazel is bent back on itself it will break but if given a turn and a twist the fibres remain unbroken. This action requires a particular knack and an iron-hand grip whilst the hazel must be young and newly cut to have the necessary suppleness. When a few thin rods have been woven the process is continued with cleft hazel which has been split with a bill hook with a razor-sharp edge. The lacing is kept tight either by pushing down with the foot or banging it with the back of the bill hook. When the final height has been reached the hurdle is removed retaining its slight curvature given by the mould. This is an important feature as it allows the wood to shrink without warping the hurdle and enables it to bind tighter as it flattens with use. The finished hurdle will show all the bark on one side and the white of the cleft hazel on the other giving a very pleasing, well-finished appearance. An average of four or five hurdles can be made in a day.

A hurdle maker requires about 3 acres of coppiced hazel per year and if lucky he will have about 28 acres of coppice which he works over every seven or eight years while the oak trees continue to grow overhead.

All the work takes place in the open so that it is held up if the weather conditions become too bad. In this case time is not lost, because then it can be spent under cover cutting hazel spars for thatchers.

BAR HURDLES

Bar or gate hurdles are used for a variety of jobs around the farm such as making temporary pens for sheep or calves or plugging holes in fences. Nowadays most of the output goes for making horse-jumps, the size and construction varying with the requirement.

There is no modern substitute to beat the hand-made cleft ash hurdle for strength and durability.

The best wood for the purpose is cut during the winter from stools or coppice wood between sixteen and twenty-five years of age. Wood of this type is becoming increasingly hard to obtain and this is one of the difficulties facing the craftsman. As an alternative, sweet chestnut is a satisfactory substitute. The modern power-saw is a great help to the woodsman and speeds up his work considerably. For preference the wood should be free from knots though small ones do not matter. If they are large, the wood can be used as fencing stakes.

The wood is normally cut to the required lengths when felled, as this facilitates handling and transport, thus saving both time and money.

When required the ash poles are clamped in a wooden horse and

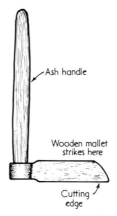

Ash handle

Wooden mallet
strikes here

Cutting
edge

A froe for cleaving wood

30

split with a fromard or froe, a type of axe that is struck on the head with a wooden mallet or belter. This causes it to split and by moving the handle of the fromard horizontally the wood is cleft along the length of the grain so that maximum strength is ensured. By repeating the process, clefts of the required thickness are obtained, the wood always being split whilst still green. The clefts are next trimmed with a draw knife and the bark removed to prevent water hanging underneath and eventually causing it to rot.

Slightly different techniques are required for the various types of hurdles. Those for sheep have six horizontal bars with the lower ones closer together so that lambs cannot get through. These bars have tenons at each end which fit into mortice holes in the two vertical end bars and alternative bars are fixed with an easily removable nail making it a simple job to renew any piece that becomes split or broken due to carelessness or an accident.

A vertical bar is clinch-nailed down the centre of the hurdle and two sloping bars added to give it rigidity.

Sheep hurdles are 6 feet long and 3 feet 6 inches high and two men can turn out a dozen a day once the timber has been cut and transported.

Hurdles for horse-jumps are more rugged and made of slightly heavier timber as they frequently get knocked and even broken. The horizontal bars do not protrude through the end ones as the hurdles sometimes have to be fitted close to each other. The end bars are pinned to the horizontal with wooden dowel pins. Mortices are quickly made by boring two holes about $\frac{1}{2}$ inch in diameter 2 inches apart and gouging out the intervening wood with a morticing tool. Jumping-hurdles are normally 6 feet long and 5 feet 2 inches high whilst those for school are a little lower. These hurdles are frequently interlaced with birch branches which are cut off at the required height.

Hurdles normally last for five or six years though this very much depends on their use and how they are looked after. There is little wastage as odd ends or unsatisfactory timber is cut into logs, ash being one of the best firewoods burning hot and clean.

OSIER HURDLES

A type of hurdle that is made in small quantities is constructed of osiers. First a number of posts, whose length depends on the required height of the hurdle up to 6 feet, are clamped in a vertical position about 9 inches apart. These posts are usually of willow though hazel and ash do equally well. Bands of osiers, wetted to make them supple are slewed between the verticals about eight at a time. The top and bottom rows are usually finished with a row of waling in stouter rods to hold the work together.

On removal from the clamp the end verticals are pointed so they can be put in the ground and the remainder of the verticals trimmed to give a neat appearance. These hurdles are used for general purposes in such places as gardens to give privacy whilst new hedges are growing, and are usually made from the rougher types of osier, which would otherwise be wasted.

CHARCOAL BURNING

Charcoal burning is one of the most ancient of woodland crafts. It is made by burning wood and excluding air so that combustion does not take place. The residue left consists of a little wood ash and a lot of logs that have been burned to carbon.

The traditional method of making it was in stacks out in the woods. The families pursuing this trade tended to be solitary and shy, living in earth huts in the woods and moving to a new area after about eighteen months or so when wood supplies were exhausted in the place they were working. This was the charcoal burners' way of life until a few years ago, but I doubt if any are now left carrying on a life like this.

Skill, care and vigilance were needed to produce a successful end product. To make a stack, first a chimney was constructed of wood. Round this logs were placed forming an ever-widening circle on the ground and built up to a tumulus about 6 feet high and 30 feet in diameter. This was then covered over with a thatch of such material as bracken, straw or nettles and finally a layer of sifted earth 4 or 5

The old type of clamp in the course of construction. It will finally be covered with earth

A two-piece kiln in the process of firing

inches thick. This layer excluded all air and had to be kept in good repair when burning took place. To start burning, some ignited charcoal was dropped down the chimney to commence the operation which continued for several days. At first white smoke was emitted being mostly due to the moisture from the wood followed by a blue haze as the by-products, consisting of wood alcohol and tar, were dissipated into the atmosphere. At the crucial moment, which only experience could tell, the top of the stack was sealed and the burning continued slowly for several days with the operator in continual attendance. The main enemies were wind, making it burn too quickly, or a leak in the outer casing of earth. This had to be mended at once or all would burn to ash.

When burning was completed the earth was removed for re-use, caution being essential to avoid spoiling the charcoal inside. A good burn left much of the wood in the shape of the original log. Considerable care had to be taken so that there was no ignition when unloading the stack and some water was always at hand to extinguish any flare-up.

Charcoal finishes up weighing about a sixth of the weight of the original wood. In days of old it was used for smelting and glass-making, as an ingredient of gunpowder (alder wood being best for this), and now for filtering gas masks, in artificial silk, paint, dog biscuits, fertilisers and a host of other uses such as barbecue fuel and for starting Aga fires. It burns with twice the heat of wood with a short flame and no smoke.

THE PRESENT WOODLAND METHOD

Nowadays the woodsman makes charcoal in a metal kiln which is far quicker than the traditional stack method. Any wood is used but preferably when it is several months old and has lost some of its moisture. In this condition it will burn more satisfactorily. Beech and oak are preferred but elm, ash, birch, chestnut and holly are all burnt if they happen to come along. The wood is generally cord wood, consisting of all that is left over after the timber merchant has used the main trunk of a tree. To load up ready for burning, the wood is placed in the lower half of a kiln which consists of a circular cylinder about 30 inches high and with a diameter of approximately 8 feet. This has eight holes around the bottom for starting the burning and regulating the draught. First a tunnel is made from one of these holes by placing two 4 foot logs one foot apart and putting brands across them. Brands consist of stumps of wood burnt around the outside but not right through, and when starting up a new fire they ignite easily.

After the cylinder has been filled another one is placed on top of the first and the operation continues till the whole is full right up. It takes about half an hour to load up the kiln and then a metal lid is placed over the top. The eight holes around the base of the kiln are opened up by scraping earth and ashes away, a rag soaked in paraffin is lit and put into the tunnel and the wood starts burning. It goes on for between thirty and forty-eight hours depending on the conditions. During this time the draught is regulated to get a good even burn by closing the holes at the bottom of the cylinder. This is where experience counts in assessing the position by feeling the side of the kiln and regulating the draught as necessary by blocking or unblocking the holes around the base. The main enemies are wind and rain during the night when the burning kiln is left unattended. A strong wind can cause it to burn too quickly and instead of charcoal there will be wood ash. This happens on very rare occasions. Heavy rain can clog the draught holes and extinguish the fire. However, it can be relit and there is no loss of material.

If all goes well when experience has adjudged that the wood has burnt to charcoal correctly, the draught holes are sealed with earth and so are the joints round the two metal cylinders and the roof cap. This makes everything airtight and all that can be seen is a blue haze escaping here and there.

About a day later, or when required, the kiln can be unloaded and the charcoal shovelled out on to a riddle or sieve, graded into sizes and put into sacks. Occasionally it is sold by the sack but generally by weight. Beech is most satisfactory for retaining its weight while some wood, like ash and fir, loses a lot.

An aggravating drawback to the operators is the fact that the fumes given off during burning rot their clothing very quickly. To their annoyance, the tax authorities' concession was minimal.

This way of making charcoal is still profitable though somewhat wasteful due to the loss of by-products given off during the burning. This defect is overcome when charcoal is made in the more modern distillation plants which may soon completely eliminate the woodland worker.

WALKING-STICKS

Walking-sticks, thumb-sticks and shepherds' crooks have always been made and used by countrymen. Most of the rural folk made their own and the fashioning of them has nearly always been a sideline for such people as shepherds who cut and carved them for beer money and sold them at the sheep fairs.

The few craftsmen who make them as a business have facilities for steaming and grow saplings specially for the purpose, ash and sweet chestnut being favoured. Chestnut is cut from two- or three-year-old coppice wood that has grown straight and free from knots. Ash sticks can be similarly grown though the best ones have a handle that has been grown to the required shape. To obtain these, young seedlings are cultivated in a plantation and when a year or two of age they are transplanted into a trench and laid over at an angle. The terminal bud is removed and the upward growth continued from a side bud thus making a right angle that forms the handle after another three or four years' growth.

If the crook of the handle is to be formed by steaming, the sticks are placed in a bed of damp sand and heated up by a boiler underneath. The wood is made pliant and is easily bent to shape. The bark will remain on the stick provided it has been seasoned properly—a process which takes about a year.

Part-time stick makers normally do not have steaming tanks so look for their raw material in woods and hedgerows using hazel, ash, blackthorn and holly for the most part.

Some of this material is to be found in hedgerows where a neglected hedge that has one time been hand laid may have branches rising vertically. By cutting off suitable ones together with a piece of the main stem a good natural handle can be obtained. At other times a length of hazel can be cut with part of its root or stem which is later fashioned into a handle or crook. Hazel bark has a very attractive colour that varies with each individual stick whilst holly goes a golden colour when treated with linseed oil after the bark has been removed. More rarely a length of wood is found that has become entwined with honeysuckle to give it a barley-sugar appearance. These are much sought after as curiosities.

All wood for sticks is cut during the winter months. The sticks need a year to season and care has to be taken that they do not warp during this period. This may be achieved by tying the stick to a piece of straight wood and hanging it vertically.

During this period the knob that will form the handle may develop some seasoning cracks, so it is necessary to cut a generous amount of wood in the first place to allow for wastage.

When ready to be worked the handle end is held in a vice and formed to shape by sawing, rasping and filing, with the craftsman using his experience and skill to obtain the best final result taking into account any knots in the wood and the curvature of the grain. The best bits can be made into shepherds' crooks which are preferred by some shepherds to the harsher wrought-iron metal ones. Having made the curve of the crook a notch is cut in the end to give the characteristic finish.

After the crook or handle has been skilfully fashioned into shape it is carefully rubbed down and polished to bring out the best in the grain and finally given half a dozen coats of polyurethane varnish for the finishing sparkle. Each stick takes between five and eight hours to make depending on its complexity.

Some walking-stick producers use straight shafts and add their own handles of deer or ram's horn, the former being used mainly by Scottish makers.

One handle can be made from each ram's horn. This has to be

Antlers and rams' horns to be made into handles for walking-sticks

first sawn to the right dimensions then bent straight by boiling for several hours. Thereafter it is formed into shape using rasps, sandpaper, glass and lastly bone to give it the final smoothness and bring out the full beauty. A hole is drilled in the horn and the shaft of the stick glued in to it possibly with a small deer-antler collar for a finish.

Many people buy the sticks so that they themselves can carve the ends of the handle or the bulbous knob in the case of blackthorn.

Stick making is taken more seriously further north in the country. Scotland has its own association and in the Lake District competitions are held at most of the agricultural shows. Elsewhere in England the individual makers exhibit their wares in a non-competitive way.

CRICKET BATS

With a big, steady and assured demand for willow for making cricket bats, the growing of willow trees has become increasingly specialised with nothing haphazard about it. There are a very large number of willow hybrids but only one is accepted by the bat manufacturers and that is *Salix alba* variety *caerulea*.

The majority of these willows come from Suffolk and Essex where the conditions suit them. They need a fairly rich and moist soil which must not be waterlogged with stagnant water. Most are grown in commercial plantations though many landowners plant a few if the right conditions are available—for instance along the banks of streams. They are propagated mostly by unrooted sets about 8 feet long which are cut from stools and pushed into the ground at least 30 feet apart.

They must be as straight as possible and not allowed to grow side shoots, the buds being rubbed off in the early stages. The alternative but lesser-used method is to take cuttings and plant them out when rooted. The trees are ready for cutting between twelve and eighteen years of age when they have a girth of about 50 inches. Some growers cut off their tops in an effort to produce a thick bole in a shorter time. A bole with a height of 10 feet can be sawn into four lengths called rounds from which the bat's clefts will be split.

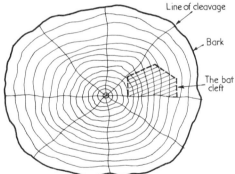

Section through a round of a tree trunk with fifteen armed growth rings, showing the position of the bat cleft

The cleaving is done using a large wooden wedge and mallet, first splitting the round in half and then cleaving into segments, about eight being produced from each round so that an average tree gives thirty-two clefts. Cleaving is done fairly quickly after felling when the wood is still green. A straight-grained tree gives a good piece of raw material. Only sap wood is used for bats so the centre few inches of heartwood are disposed of and also the outermost inch or two of growth which is soft and immature.

The ideal clefts are completely free from blemishes, have perfectly straight wide grain, and are white and stain free.

The clefts then have to be seasoned before use, preferably under natural conditions, but they can be dried in a warm chamber. In the seasoning process they may split a little at the ends and their length of 2 feet 4 inches allows for a small amount of wastage. It is at this stage that the manufacturer usually comes and selects his clefts calling on his expert eye and experience.

Some clefts are now exported to Australia where a bat-making industry has started and some are produced in Pakistan using locally grown willow which is not of the same quality of that grown in England. Otherwise all cricket-playing countries use English bats. With the demand steadily increasing more willows will have to be grown and as they take at least twelve years to mature the future needs will have to be accurately anticipated. At present a good tree is worth about £15 to £20.

Over the last 100 years the production of cricket bats has increased enormously and during this time the making of them has transferred itself from the rural craftsmen to the factory with as much mechanisation as possible, although certain of the operations continue to defy the march of progress and still call for individual craftsmanship. By the use of jigs a good deal of skilled work can be eliminated and several operations can be performed by a workman of average intelligence. Although the old-time craftsman could do all operations making a bat from start to finish, the tendency now is for the different parts of the job each to be made by a specialist.

At a very early stage it was found that willow was the most satisfactory wood to use. It is very light for its volume and is strong and resilient and so far no suitable substitute has been found, unlike the wood used for some other sports such as golf, where steel shafts have supplanted the hickory, or tennis where the ash frame has been replaced by a laminated or steel one, and hockey where a mulberry head has supplanted that of ash.

The bat-making manufacture is now dominated by a few giants, but here and there a few small businesses continue to survive.

The procuring and supply of willow is normally done by merchants. This means that the small man orders his material when he wants it and does not have to keep a large amount of money locked up in keeping big stocks. The wood that eventually makes the blade of the bat is usually supplied in clefts of about 28-inch length with a triangular cross section. Some of the clefts are kiln dried so that it is possible for a tree to be converted into a bat in a matter of days. For making a bat there has to be between 10 and 15 per cent of moisture left so after kiln drying the ends of the clefts are usually dipped in wax to retain this amount.

To make a bat the cleft has its ends cut off to reduce it to $22\frac{1}{2}$ inches if a full-sized one is required. A reason for the loss of just over 2 inches from each end is because the cleft develops slight splits or shakes at the extremities which must be cut off. Having obtained the right length the cleft is placed in a variety of jigs: the first cuts it to the correct width, the next slightly rounds the face, the next shapes the back, then the shoulder of the bat is turned on a lathe. The cleft is then roughly in the form of the finished blade. The V-shaped groove to take the splice is accurately cut on a band saw and all is ready for the fitting of the cane handle.

The handle is made up of the best cane which comes from the Borneo and Malaya area. About four sections are glued together interleaved with rubber to give it some spring and stop any jarring though the rubber insertions do not extend down the part that will eventually form the actual splice. This length of glued-up cane and rubber is turned on a lathe to the required diameter after which the splice is cut by using a jig and a circular saw. When the handle is placed in the V of the bat blade the fit should be very exact and tight. The two parts are then glued together ready for the final operation of finishing.

The finisher using a draw-knife starts by cleaning up around the

splice on the bat face, then turns it over and puts the finishing touches to the back, rounding off any roughness, leaving it beautifully smooth. Finally the shoulder is trimmed. The finisher takes about a quarter of an hour for each bat and the completed article depends largely upon his touch and skill. The bat is then looking very clean and quite white but to make it pure white a bleaching solution is applied by brush which removes or reduces any brown stains in the wood, an important factor when it comes to selling. The face of the bat is still comparatively soft, too much so for use, so it is subjected to a pressure of about 1 ton which depresses the surface by about $\frac{1}{4}$ inch.

All that now remains are the finishing touches: the thread binding around the handle, the rubber handle glued on, the maker's name applied and the etceteras such as 'Super Grade' followed by a lot of stars and possibly the stamped autograph of a famous player. There is no doubt that the appearance has a big effect on the selling of the product and even moderate players seem able to afford the top quality.

A certain number of blemishes may appear in the making, such as a slight knot, grain not perfectly straight, or some discoloration that will not bleach out. In such cases the bat cannot sell as a top-quality article and has to be downgraded. It takes the same time and skill to make one whatever its quality so those not in the top grade are probably manufactured at a loss.

The only two dimensions that a bat has to comply with, according to the rules are that 'The bat shall not exceed $4\frac{1}{4}$ inches in the widest part, it shall not be more than 38 inches in length.'

CHAPTER 2

WHEELWRIGHTING

THE WHEELWRIGHT

UP TILL the early part of the present century every community had its wheelwright but since then the craft has disappeared at a faster rate than almost any other. Its demise has been caused chiefly by the internal combustion engine taking over from the horse and the arrival of factory-made mass-produced trailers with pneumatic wheels.

Trailers and wheels flooded the market immediately after the war when army surplus vehicles were sold with the effect of killing off overnight the businesses of the remaining wheelwrights. Beautifully built waggons and carts fetched no more than £1 at auctions so that it was a waste of time sending them to be sold and nobody had a new one made.

A wheelwright always had more work in the summer than the winter. Farmers rarely had their vehicles overhauled till the spring when there was a rush to get them ready. Winter was the time to build new vehicles and to cut and hew wood roughly to the required shape before leaving it to season.

The wood used was almost entirely oak, elm, beech or ash, and later this quartet was joined by imported deal.

The owner of the business usually preferred to select his own timber from the growing tree. Very few parts of a waggon are straight and a shrewd man bought trees with the right curves that would serve his purpose. Woodland trees were preferred as those in the hedgerows tended to be knotty and liable to have wire or nails embedded in them which damaged the saws.

The disadvantage of a wheelwright carrying a stock of timber was the fact that a great deal of money was locked up for a number of years and he may not have had the capital or the room to afford this luxury. Instead the timber might be bought from a dealer at a higher price, a practice that had its advantages as the wood could be carefully examined for knots and blemishes before purchase.

Trees were always felled in winter when they were in the dormant stage and they were brought in and left to season for anything up to ten years.

The economic cutting of wood to use it to the best advantage and to avoid waste played a significant part in the financial success of the business.

CARTS AND WAGGONS

The difference between a cart and a waggon is that the former had two wheels and the latter four. Their design altered very little over the centuries so they did not become obsolete. The bodies probably outlived several sets of wheels and as every bit was easily renewable it was possible for a supposedly hundred-year-old vehicle to have none of its original parts.

During the latter part of the last century, waggons and wheels began to be produced in factories, to the detriment of the wheelwright. In order to compete the latter had to cut out refinements and use machine-sawn wood and metal fittings so that the vehicles took on a plainer and more austere look.

Carts with their two wheels were much lighter and less complicated in construction than waggons and considerably cheaper to build. There was no intricate gear for steering and they were much more manoeuvrable and therefore used whenever possible.

Unlike waggons they could be constructed so as to be able to tip, and were used for all odd jobs like hauling dung and root crops.

The bottom boards originally ran longitudinally and were called 'long boards' and were generally made of elm. In later years cheaper deal cross boarding was frequently substituted to save expense. The sides were wider at the back than the front in a tipping cart so that the load slid out more easily. Some carts had a crank axle enabling the body to be built lower—a feature of milk floats.

The shafts were rigidly fixed to the cart unlike those of a waggon which were pivoted so the load had to be carefully balanced to make it comfortable for the horse. Two wheels caused less friction than the four of a waggon and they could be made larger up to about 5 feet in diameter enabling them to ride rough ground more easily.

A good waggon demonstrated all the best virtues of the wheelwright craft, and very beautiful and graceful they were, especially if no expense was spared. They had few straight lines, most of the wood being gently curved and all surplus pared away with a spokeshave to keep the waggon as light as possible without impairing the strength. The weight could be reduced in this manner by about one-eighth.

Carts and waggons were gaily painted in the traditional colours of the district with red, royal blue and buff predominating.

Surprisingly few nails were used. Most of the tenon joints were held in place by oak pins, and coach bolts were used extensively.

One of the most important features of a waggon was the turning-circle or lock and this governed the size of the front wheels which were always smaller than those at the back. The lock could be quarter, half, three-quarters and full. A quarter lock had comparatively large front wheels which only turned a very limited amount before coming up against the turning cletes on the side of the waggon, a feature that severely limited its use. To improve

This abandoned quarter-lock waggon has wide wheels needing both a tyre and a strake. It had a large turning-circle

matters a waggon with a waisted bed was devised which enabled the wheels to turn a bit more and this was termed a half lock.

A three-quarter lock waggon had smaller front wheels which turned under the waggon till they met the pole joining the front and rear axle beds. A full lock meant the wheels could turn right round and was useful for such vehicles as brewers' drays and millers' waggons.

Small wheels had a number of disadvantages. They did not ride pot holes or undulations very well and had much less clearance making them more liable to become stuck in a deeply rutted lane, though they were quite satisfactory for road work.

A waggon was made in two parts, the undercarriage and the main body. They were bolted together at the back whilst the king pin kept the front together, at the same time allowing the front pair of wheels to turn.

The wheels were fitted on axles that were originally of wood with metal pieces let in to take the wear and later of iron which was let in to a cross beam called an axle bed. The axles were tilted downwards at a slight angle which compensated for the dish and brought the spoke to a vertical position at the moment it was carrying the weight. As an added refinement the front wheels had a slight toe in.

The bodies of waggons varied a good deal, depending on their use and the district. For instance millers had them with high boarded sides whilst sometimes the sides were like skeletons without boarding to save weight. Others had outraves which were built out over the wheels. Most attractive of all were the hoop-raved waggons where the outrave curved gracefully over the large back wheels.

A waggon sometimes overturned and when this occurred it probably snapped the king pin and possibly broke a shaft. The simple-looking shafts were most carefully shaped, wide at the back, curved in by the collar and then turned outwards. A broken one could often be spliced on the spot using metal bands.

Every waggon had a few fittings for braking and stopping. A drug bat, skid pan or slipper was a shoe attached to a chain that was put under one of the back wheels which then skidded and acted as a brake when going downhill. A locking chain was a length of chain that was passed through the wheel to stop it turning.

For going up hill there was the roller scotch, a cylinder of wood (usually elm) with iron bands that rolled along an inch or two behind the rear wheel and came into use if the waggon began to roll backwards. There was also the dog-stick consisting of a stick with one end attached to the cart and the other end fitted with a prong that dug itself in if the cart started to go backwards.

When tractors replaced horses some waggons were adapted for towing but they did not take kindly to the higher speeds and were soon shaken to bits. Thus they quickly became obsolete after having remained supreme for hundreds of years.

THE WHEELS

The invention of the wheel was one of man's most valuable discoveries. It had to be very strong and cleverly made to stand up to the stresses and strains imposed upon it.

The earliest wheels were of solid wood, usually several pieces joined together and rimmed with leather. Lighter spoked wheels followed with iron rims and this type held its own for hundreds of years. The making of them was the most intricate part of the wheelwright's job.

The hub of the wheel, called the stock, was invariably made of elm because of its tough grain. At the turn of the century, metal stocks made their appearance and increased in number. The stock had slots drilled in it to take the spokes of which there could be any number from six to fourteen. There was always an even number to take the ash felloes that formed the rim of the wheel.

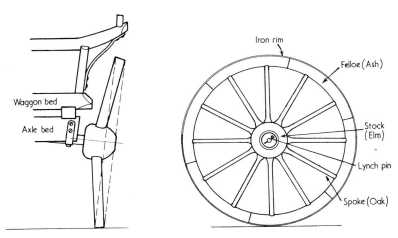

A waggon wheel

All wheels for horse-drawn vehicles had an essential feature called dish. This meant that the spokes sloped slightly outward from the hub. A plodding horse gave a pull with a sideways thrust first to the near and then to the offside wheel. This dish helped to absorb the continual battering. By making the axle with a slightly downward tilt, the weight on the wheel (which could be three-quarters of a ton) came over the spoke when it was in a vertical position. It also meant that the top of the wheel sloped outwards allowing the vehicle to be built a little wider.

The spokes were made with heart of oak which was split when green and left to season for some years before being carefully shaped to the required size.

The felloes, pronounced fellies, were the curved pieces that formed the wheel rim. They were cut out of hardwood, usually ash, either by circular saw or an adze for the inside and an axe outside. Two holes were drilled in exactly the right place to take the top of the spokes and the ends were bored to take dowels of oak or sometimes metal.

Fitting the felloes on the spokes posed a problem. They had all

A samson bar pulling two spokes together so that the last felloe can be fitted

to be put on together and not singly and when placed around the wheel made a greater diameter than the finished article. The ends of a pair of spokes had to be forced together slightly with a tool called a spoke dog or samson bar so they would come opposite the holes in the felloes. The felloes were first just tapped on all round the wheel and as this operation progressed the dowels in the ends moved in to the appropriate holes. The felloes were then hammered down tight. For protection they needed to be shod and this took the form of a tyre, a continuous hoop of metal or a number of short curved bars called strakes or possibly a combination of both if the wheel was very wide.

The circumference of the wheel was measured using an instrument called a traveller consisting of a revolving measuring wheel about 6 inches in diameter. For a tyre a piece of metal was cut off, bent in a circle and welded up. It was essential for its final diameter to be an inch or so less than the wheel in order to bind tight when shrunk on.

Strakes came into general use earlier than the continuous tyre and were easier to put on. The metal used for both tyres and strakes was about $\frac{3}{4}$ inch thick, up to 4 inches wide and weighed about a hundredweight. The width of the tyre depended on the type of vehicle and could be as much as 9 inches in which case it would have two rows, either strakes or one hoop tyre and a set of strakes.

For tyring, the wheel was screwed down flat on a specially made bed and the tyre heated in a fire till red hot. It was then removed, carried to the tyring bed and put over the wheel and hammered on. It needed at least three men for this operation, two to carry the tyre using metal fire-dogs and the third man to hammer the tyre on to the wheel. This had to be done inside two minutes or the tyre would set the wood of the wheel alight. As soon as it was on, water, which was previously placed on hand, was poured over the wheel. Clouds of steam arose and the wood cracked ominously as the joints and dowels were forced in tight by the shrinking metal which caused the wheel to take on a little extra dish.

Strakes were also heated in a fire and nailed on while hot, but this was a less spectacular process than tyring.

At some stage of making the wheel a hole was bored in the stock to take a metal tube called an axle box which was wedged in and eventually took the axle.

The repair of wheels accounted for the greater part of a wheelwright's work, particularly in the summer when carts and waggons were used more and the dry weather shrank the wood, allowing the tyre to become loose. The old carters liked to drive through a stream to get the wheels wet and prevent the wood shrinking. A loose tyre could often be repaired by half a day's work reducing the diameter an inch and shrinking it back on.

There are a number of ceremonial coaches, brewers' drays and show carriages that are still used and need a wheelwright from time to time, but sadly the number still in business is very few indeed.

A wheelwright's tools, including an elm stock, a traveller, an axle box (right) and an adze

CHAPTER 3

COOPERING

COOPERING IS the name of the craft of making wooden casks or barrels and is one of the most difficult in which to obtain any degree of proficiency. The craft goes back several thousand years. Casks were frequently used for packaging materials, but the main requirement was to carry liquid, in particular wine and beer. Perfection is required for a cask to be completely watertight and considering that everything is done by eye an extraordinary amount of skill is needed. In some crafts a sub-standard article may still have its use but for a wooden cask only the top quality is acceptable.

A variety of different woods can be used, sometimes chestnut though best of all is oak. There is a surprising range in the quality of oak, depending partly on the soil in which the tree grows and partly on the variety. An excess of branches makes the wood knotty. English oak is rather stringy and much of it is unsuitable for cask making, so in spite of the amount grown, most casks are made from imported wood from America, Japan or Persia. None, however, surpasses that from the Baltic, frequently referred to as Memel oak, though this is now no longer obtainable.

Unfortunately the wooden cask is being rapidly replaced by those of metal or plastic for beer and cider, although for wine and spirits wood is at present holding its own.

In England the craft has declined drastically. A comparatively small number of new casks are made, mostly in a few factories that supply the remaining breweries that use them. These have coopers who are employed almost exclusively on repairs. The larger breweries regard wooden casks as a nuisance so that those that have them are mostly the smaller concerns who claim to have built up a clientele of connoisseurs of beer who prefer to drink it straight from the wood. There is a thriving organisation called The Society for the Preservation of Beers from the Wood amongst whose aims are to eschew the drinking of beer from 'sealed dustbins' and to promote the drinking of beer from wooden barrels.

Oak for barrels comes from the heartwood of a mature tree that will have taken over a 100 years to grow to the required dimensions. The wood is sawn into logs which are then cleft into billets from which wood for the staves is produced preferably by cleaving, though nowadays probably cut by saw after the removal of the sap wood. The direction in which the grain runs is most important and it is essential that the annular growth rings run from the back to the front of the staves and not along the width.

Barrels are made in a large variety of sizes each with their own particular name like hogsheads, kilderkins, firkins, pins, etc. The volume of liquid they hold is a standard amount with allowance made for a slight variation as it is impossible to be exact in making them. In addition the volume they hold decreases in use partly because the hoops are hammered down harder from time to time causing the barrel to lose some of its bulge and a few pints of capacity.

The cooper's tools are mostly peculiar to the trade, particularly

(Opposite) Planing a groove on a barrel to take the head

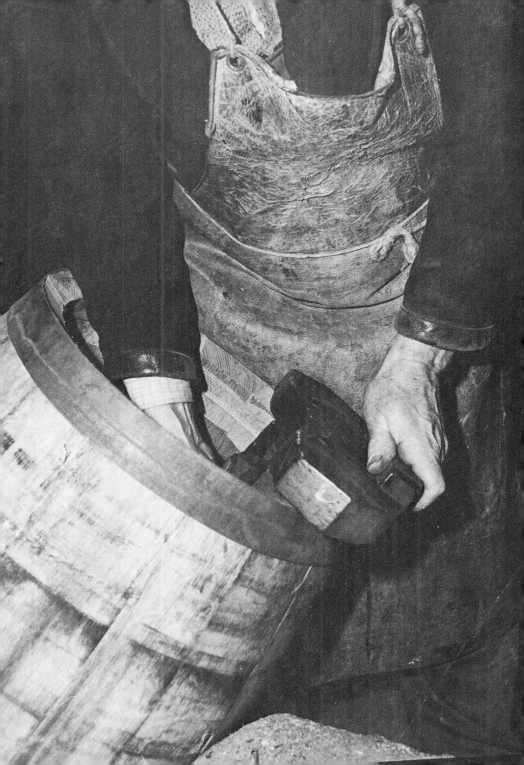

in the case of the planes, most of which are shaped to work inside the circular barrel and to cut grooves to take the caps. The planes are mostly of beechwood and can be bought, although the likelihood is that the cooper either made them himself when an apprentice or inherited them. Craftsmen look after their tools with the utmost care, keeping them razor sharp and treating them as old friends so it is not unusual to come across one 100 years old.

Some of the operations of barrel making have been mechanised though much of the work is still done individually. This is entirely so with repairs which account for most of the cooper's time.

To make a stave, a length of oak of the required dimensions is taken. With an axe the cooper trims away with great accuracy some of the wood on the sides and towards both ends to give it a taper. It is next put on the jointer and planed at an angle with an incredible degree of skill. The jointer consists of a long sloping beechwood plane fixed in position with the blade uppermost. The plane remains stationary and the stave is passed to and fro across the cutting blade at a slight angle in order to give it the necessary bevel so that it will fit correctly in place as a member of the circular radius of the completed cask. Each stave then has to be slightly hollowed on the inside with a special knife and some wood removed from the back with a backing knife. When the correct number of staves have been made in this manner they are raised together and held in a vertical position by a series of trussing hoops that are made of ash or iron and are forced down to hold the staves in position. Next follows the operation of trussing in which the staves are made pliable either by placing the cask in a steaming chest or by lighting a fire of oak shavings inside the cask. Trusses of various sizes are forced on and the cask assumes its characteristic shape whilst the staves remain set in their curved state as the wood dries out. In heating up the staves by fire it is important for the chippings to be of oak as coal or other wood might impregnate the cask and taint the beer.

The ends of the staves are squared off using an adze to form the chime. Meanwhile the heads of the cask have to be made. These are formed with a number of sections dowelled together and shaped to form a circle. Using one of the specially curved planes, a groove is made inside the barrel all the way round to take the heads. The rim of the latter has the edge bevelled on one face to reduce its thickness before being placed in the grooves made for it, the chime hoop is then forced on making an almost exact fit. If caulking is necessary, this is done by forcing in some bulrushes.

A number of additional refinements go into the making of a cask. For instance the head at one end has the grain running at right angles to that at the other, the joints on the top set of hoops face the opposite way to those below and the stave that takes the bung is slightly larger and stronger than the rest. The hole for the bung is made by an auger and a circular metal piece is let in the hole to take the wooden bung and to prevent wear. Finally the tap hole is made in one of the heads and the cask is ready for use.

If properly maintained it will have a life of forty years or more, possibly as much as sixty, though careless handling can reduce this time greatly. Care has to be taken not to leave empty casks on end with the open tap hole uppermost. Rain or other impurities can collect in the top, run down inside, and in a short time ruin the wood and turn it into a 'stinker' fit only to be burnt.

On return to the brewery all casks have to be steam sterilised before they are refilled.

The most vulnerable parts are the chimes which can easily get broken, necessitating the renewal of a complete stave. This entails a lengthy job taking the cask to bits.

The other common fault is for old barrels to lose an unacceptable amount of their capacity. To rectify this one of the staves has to be replaced with a slightly larger one. The cask may be given an increased bulge, alternatively a larger pair of heads can be fitted.

More maintenance is generally needed in the summer when leaks are more common. The contents may expand if the cask is left in the sun causing leaks.

The craft is at present in a very precarious position. Wooden casks need continuous maintenance by very skilled men whereas metal ones need far less and are easier to handle.

CHAPTER 4

THE SMITH

WROUGHT-IRON WORK

THE VILLAGE smith was, until about thirty years ago, a vital member of any rural community and to be found in most villages even those with comparatively small populations. He was a man of great versatility undertaking every metal job that came his way. First there were the essential ones such as repairing farm machinery and shoeing horses, these having priority over all else. At other times he would turn his hand to such tasks as making fire grates, pokers, door-hinges, gates, etc. Over the last few decades the demand for his work has become progressively less, because of a drop in the horse population, coupled with the mass production of farm implements and machinery, so that when anything breaks, it is replaced by a new factory-made spare part.

Here and there a few enterprising blacksmiths have survived and are prospering though their prices remain modest and they do not become as rich as they deserve. They are rewarded by the pride in their craftsmanship and the satisfaction derived from a well-executed job. They have a great variety of work so never become bored or stale nor are they subjected to many of the stresses of modern life.

The centre piece of their place of work is the forge where the glowing fire is brought to the necessary heat by a blower. The older ones are worked by a large pair of leather hand-bellows which have steadily been replaced by the easily controlled, electric-driven fan that brings the fire into use in about ten minutes.

Along the front of the forge is the quenching trough containing water to cool either the piece of metal being worked or the tools.

The fuel varies. It is usually a mixture of coal and coke graded into small pieces. The smith has to find out by trial and error the mixture that suits him best that can be obtained from his local coal merchant. For hand work, wrought iron is rarely if ever used, being difficult to obtain now the smelting processes have changed, so that most work is done in best black mild steel bar. This is preferred by some because it is produced in an even quality and can be worked cold for some jobs.

Most of the work is done with hot metal heated to a very exact temperature making it pliable and easy to fashion, the temperature being judged by experience. Too high a temperature might melt the metal which has to be brought to a heat that causes it to change colour as it gets hotter passing through stages of black, purple, cherry red to white. Speed and accuracy are essential during the short time it is at the correct heat to be worked. Frequently it has to be returned to the fire to restore the heat.

Much of the work is done on an anvil fixed to a wooden block usually of elm which sets it at the right height and allows a degree of spring. The anvil has a flat surface in the middle, a beak at one end and a number of holes at the other into which are placed a variety of tools depending on the object that is being made. The tools being used have to be placed handy so that no time is lost when the metal is brought from the forge. Most of the work is done using a hammer of which there are a wide variety of types. Care has to be taken that cinders or impurities are not hammered into the article. When completed it will show no sign of any hammer marks if skilfully done.

Besides hammers other essential tools are tongs, cutting chisels, vices and a wide variety of swages for drawing out bars, fullers, shears, scroll formers in various sizes, etc. A large number of these will have been made by the blacksmith himself so that the size of the collection and the variety depend on the individual. Many a skilled man tries to keep these down to a minimum and to rely on his dexterity to produce the desired effects.

The work is preponderantly hand made with some mechanisation for power-drilling holes and cutting. A lot of the pieces are riveted together, with the rivet heads being countersunk for appearance sake. Alternatively clips may be used or better still pieces may be welded together with almost invisible joins.

When it comes to making an article such as a wrought-iron gate the blacksmith may be presented with a design or he might produce one himself. The most satisfactory solution is for the craftsman and client to get together and evolve it so that the blacksmith is not forced to produce something with which he is not in sympathy. There are books of designs which can be copied if required though most people who can afford it prefer to be original.

In the past, with a few notable exceptions, blacksmiths have been rustic rural craftsmen with little learning or aesthetic feeling so their work has tended to be functional, solid and reserved in design. Now they are more sophisticated and specialised in hand-wrought work turning out articles of a high artistic quality. Their ranks have recently been augmented by artists turned blacksmith who tend to produce more flamboyant and delicate designs some of which are excellent. However in all trades there is good and bad to be found. Wrought iron is no exception. Hand-made products must not be confused with the mass-produced factory specimens made of lightweight metal, flimsy in construction, containing an excess of scroll work all spot-welded together and finally dipped in a tank of gloss paint. These mostly have little artistic merit and require constant maintenance to stop rust.

Having decided upon a design, the outline in full scale is drawn with a scriber on a piece of sheet metal that has been chalked over.

60

As work progresses the pieces are assembled over this drawing and eventually joined together.

In a good design all the parts are functional adding strength to the work whilst the curved pieces such as scrolls add beauty. Everything must be precisely and visually balanced, no easy task bearing in mind the scrolls are all done by eye and have to match each other exactly having been made by bending round a scroll former when hot. The ease with which a practised blacksmith achieves this near perfection can be disarmingly deceptive.

Sometimes repoussé work is seen. This is made out of sheet metal cut out and beaten into relief from behind. The work of this type so admirably executed by the Frenchman Tijou nearly 300 years ago has never been surpassed and is still to be seen in St Paul's Cathedral and the gates at Hampton Court Palace.

Rust is the great enemy of wrought iron. Before the iron leaves the workshops, great care is taken to preserve it and there is a certain amount of secrecy about the process used. A solution based on linseed oil is brushed on and burnt in with an acetylene lamp and finished off with several coats of matt black. This is the usual finish though some customers prefer a gloss paint with a little gilding to highlight the finer points. If a work is given routine attention to avoid rust, it will last for hundreds of years. If kept indoors the necessary maintenance is negligible. An alternate finish used largely for indoor work is armour bright. To obtain this finish extreme care must be taken from the start to avoid all blemishes, the final touches being given by using very fine emery cloth followed as a rule by a coat of transparent lacquer.

Much of the work consists of repairs to such items as neglected gates, church weathercocks, garden ornaments and craftsmen's signs. The main patrons are firms and institutions requiring large prestigious entrance gates. In addition there is a steady demand for garden gates, windvanes, fire screens, and other small items that can be afforded by most people with a liking for hand-made articles. Their prices may range from £10 to £100 or upwards depending on the amount of time put into it. Labour is by far the greatest element of the cost. A blacksmith and his mate probably use 2 or 3 tons of material a year costing around £250 a ton. Overheads are not very great as a car is not essential and a telephone is a nuisance as work has to be stopped to answer it.

Most blacksmiths have a mate. A good deal can be done single-handed but for some of the bigger pieces an assistant is essential to wield the heavy hammer or help manhandle the heavier articles.

Normal care has to be taken to avoid accidents. Pieces of metal might be chipped off and hit the craftsman and it is all too easy to pick up a hot piece of metal in the hand, a lesson that usually only has to be learnt once in the early days of apprenticeship.

Good specimens of wrought iron are to be seen in a great many places particularly in churches which possess some very old work in such places as door-hinges and around tombs and screens. Some

The arbour by Robert Bakewell at Melbourne Hall in Derbyshire, one of the best pieces of British wrought-iron work

of the finest perished at the hands of the iconoclasts and puritans though luckily a lot escaped destruction.

Most great houses and universities have imposing entrance gates and frequently very good garden ornaments. Unfortunately many of the latter were swept away during the era of landscape gardening by Capability Brown in the eighteenth century. One outstanding example survived—Robert Bakewell's magnificent arbour at Melbourne Hall in Derbyshire.

It is quite surprising how most of the outstanding wrought-iron craftsmen remain anonymous and probably died poor. They invariably worked all their lives in one place.

The best craftsmen of all types tended to be foreigners who enjoyed more prestige and patronage than in this country and so tended to be a more educated and artistic type of person.

In regency times there was a vogue for cast-iron decoration, some of which is acceptably elegant and was used extensively in place of wrought-iron. It was cheaper and easier to produce though it never had the lightness and individuality of its counterpart. Sometimes the two were combined with quite pleasing results.

Wrought-iron work is now enjoying a minor boom. A skilled and reputed craftsman gets all the work he can cope with without advertising. There is a growing appreciation of genuine hand-made articles and more attention is paid to design. With a fair number of apprentices about, it looks as if the craft will more than hold its own and the prospects look reasonably good.

FARRIERY

The old-time village blacksmith was generally a jack of all trades and almost certainly well practised in farriery—the shoeing of horses. It is possible that there may have been enough horses in the district to enable him to devote all his time to farriery. Up till about 1930 every farm had cart horses, and a great variety of delivery vans for milk, bread, coal, etc., were horse-drawn. A pair of men could be kept in full employment servicing 200 horses providing they followed the usual practice of coming to the smithy. With a large number of farriers about, a horse never had to travel far in order to be shod.

Times, however, have changed very rapidly during the last half century, with the horse population becoming drastically reduced as far as agriculture is concerned though numbers kept for leisure pursuits are again on the increase. The village blacksmith had to face up to very difficult times and the majority slowly went out of business or just hung on till they retired. Many of the older men were unable to leave their forges, buy a car and become mobile. Indeed most could not afford to do so. However, the fortunate few who survived and are able to travel around now cover a very large area and are doing reasonably well. It has meant that nearly all the shoeing is done cold and much time is taken in travelling so that each farrier shoes less horses.

The old type of farrier buys his material of mild steel in strips. Pieces are cut off and fashioned into shoes of the right size and weight. Between six and eight holes are punched in each shoe to take the nails and in most cases a clip is raised. When a horse is reshod the old set of shoes are usually retained as a pattern for the next replacement set so that the minimum time is wasted. Farriers are often so busy that they buy some of the shoes ready-made in order to save time. These have to have the clip made and always have to be altered as no horses' feet are exactly standard size. Attempts are being made to produce nylon and synthetic resin shoes but so far these have not impressed the farriers.

They used to make all their own nails but as they are readily available in a variety of different sizes it is unlikely that any hand-made ones are used today.

A slightly better fit is obtained if a shoe is put on hot. The shaping is easier and the hot shoe beds in better to the horse's hoof. It is a lengthier business and slowly passing out of favour largely because the farrier cannot take his fire around with him

(Opposite) A farrier shaping a shoe on an anvil

64

though he will have a small portable forge in his car for minor adjustments.

Why are horses shod and is it necessary if they exist in the wild state without attention? In fact wild horses have trouble with their hooves and can wear them down causing soreness whilst splinters and thorns can fester and cause gangrene.

The hoof has an outer covering of horn which grows at the rate of about 1 inch in three months and has to be trimmed if the horse is pastured on soft ground and shod if doing roadwork or walking on abrasive surfaces.

When shoeing the farrier usually talks to the horse and establishes an understanding with the animal that makes his work less difficult though some horses are awkward and occasionally vicious. Though some farriers may give the horse titbits like an apple or carrot, the practice is not to be commended as the animal will always be looking for its treat.

A horse is always approached from the near side and the near front foot dealt with first, working round in an anti-clockwise direction. First the old set of shoes is removed. The farrier runs his hand down the back of the horse's leg and the animal allows it to be raised and held in between the farrier's legs which are covered with a leather apron. The hoof is then cleaned and the horn trimmed with a paring knife and rasp. Farriers prefer to work in pairs helping each other and speeding up the job and calming the horse if necessary.

After trimming the hoof the shoe is tested for fit and if all is well is fixed on using the specially shaped nails which are placed in the holes in the shoe and hammered through the horn of the hoof to emerge out of the side of the latter. There is very little margin for error and if the nail is not angled with precision it may penetrate the quick of the hoof possibly causing the horse to lash out and for ever afterwards be nervous in the presence of the farrier. The protruding nail is then clinched by snipping off the end and gently hammering over, finally being smoothed off with a rasp, care being taken not to overdo this as it might weaken the hold and the shoe would soon be cast.

A farrier always has to work in a very awkward position with his back and knees bent as he leans over the hoof so that he develops very strong muscles. Occasionally the hoof may be rested on a metal tripod to take some of the weight especially if the farrier is shoeing a heavy shire horse.

All farriers have the occasional accident. A horse can easily send him flying when the shoe is being put on and most have sustained gashes on the leg from the shoeing nail before it has been clinched over when the horse has moved unexpectedly, a comparatively frequent occurrence that may be caused by the irritating presence of flies or by sultry weather. Some farriers wear industrial shoes with steel toecaps as a safeguard against their toes being trodden on by accident.

Horses are individuals with each one having a different leg action and hoof formation which the farrier has to study very carefully. Inherent defects often can be corrected or compensated by the farrier, particularly on a young horse, and his skill can help a great deal.

The time taken to shoe a horse, four feet or 'all round' as it is called, varies. It can be as quick as half an hour but a general average is an hour, not counting the time that has been put in to make the set of shoes.

The present-day cost of shoeing is around £4 a set in addition to which the customer has to pay for the travelling time. A farrier normally works a round setting off early in the morning and often finishing late in the evening with his rate of progress governed by the snags that are encountered. It is quite impossible to work to a strict schedule.

The frequency a horse has to be shod depends on a variety of factors such as the amount of roadwork or hunting that is done. An average is three weeks to a month when working hard, and a somewhat longer period if the horse is only doing light work.

Racehorses, of which there are now 11,000 in training and breeding establishments, require special treatment. These highly strung, nervous animals, often worth many thousands of pounds,

need to be shod by the most skilled and experienced farriers. Large stables might have their own farrier, but mostly they have first call on the best man in the district. The shoeing of racehorses is always done cold.

For racing, horses have light steel or duralumin plates which are put on shortly before the race, preferably at the stables, though a farrier is in attendance at every race meeting in case of emergencies. A farrier capable of shoeing racehorses can shoe anything.

The craft is enjoying a minor boom due to the steady increase in the total horse population. It is an essential service dealing with people who can afford to pay a fair price for the work. There are a number of apprentices learning the trade and a school for them at Hereford where they are examined and passed which helps to keep the standard and improve the quality of the working farrier.

An experienced farrier can expect to earn about £1,500 a year. If he is dealing with racehorses there is often work to be done on Sunday in preparation for racing the following day. He has to possess a car and travel many miles most days. It is essential to have a telephone which in turn means there has to be somebody to answer it. Needless to say he has to have a premises with a forge which he works himself unless he employs somebody to make his shoes for him and he cannot afford to be absent for long for sickness or holidays, especially if dealing with racehorses.

The life is a hard one mentally as well as physically, as concentration is required all the time. The overheads are considerable and, at the end of it all the financial rewards of the business are not very great.

CHAPTER 5

THATCH

THATCHING WAS one of the earliest and most common forms of roof-covering from ancient times until quite recently. The materials used were close at hand and comparatively easy to work, making it the cheapest form of roofing available. A variety of different materials were used, preferably wheat straw or reed in coastal areas, though occasionally it was of bracken, heather or sedge.

The best is the reed *Phragmites communis* that grows chiefly around the coasts where conditions are suitable, most of it coming from Norfolk where it covers very large areas. When straw is used, it is invariably of wheat, though in the past rye proved satisfactory. There are two distinct methods of thatching with wheat, one is called long straw thatching and the other combed wheat reed. The use of the word reed is confusing as wheat reed has nothing to do with Norfolk reed, but takes its name from the fact that it has been threshed in a machine fitted with a reeding attachment. This threshes the corn out of the ear of wheat and leaves the stem undamaged, unlike combine harvesters which break the straw rendering it useless for thatching.

Straw for thatching has to be grown as a special crop and harvested with a binder and bailer before being reeded so that a certain amount of expensive and obsolete machinery is required for the job. The straw from winter-grown wheat is the most satisfactory as it has little or no pith.

Modern varieties of wheat tend to have short stalks with pithy insides and heavy ears, the stalks frequently being brittle due to the application of artificial fertilisers. Therefore special varieties have to be grown for thatching and whilst their wheat yield is likely to be less, this is compensated for by the increased value of the straw. Wheat for thatching is best harvested when still slightly green before the stalks get too brittle. It is then probably kept in a rick till required. A thatcher normally buys his straw from a dealer and has the exact quantity delivered direct to the site. A regular demand is likely throughout the year, though more is needed in the summer when thatching conditions are better.

Historically, thatch has always been the poor man's roofing material, being comparatively easy to lay. Nevertheless, a good deal of skill is required for a really first-class job. However, with the costs of labour rising steeply in recent years, a thatched roof is now becoming something of a luxury.

It may well cost around £500 to rethatch a small cottage, and considerably more if Norfolk reed is used. The covering may last from only fifteen years to seventy depending on the type of thatch, but it will have to be relaid eventually. Many old thatched cottages have become derelict as the owners cannot afford a new roof. However, the cottages usually have great character and, if situated in a country village, are eagerly sought after by retiring people or as weekend retreats. This new class of owner can afford to modernise them, keep the thatch in good order and have a house of some distinction with an increasing antique value.

A thatched roof inevitably has to have a fairly steep pitch of at least 50° in order that the rain will run off it satisfactorily. This means that they do not normally have a very wide span unless the roof trusses are unusually large in size. For this reason, the rooms tend to be small.

Thatch is one of the lightest of roofing materials and has excellent insulating qualities that keep a house warm in winter and cool in summer.

Gutters are rarely fitted, so generous overhanging eaves are needed to throw the rainwater clear. This has the disadvantage of keeping some of the light out of the upper windows and creating rather gloomy rooms. The large overhang causes a severe strain on the thatch if there is a strong wind, and necessitates very firm securing.

Gutters look incongruous but may be justified if a path passes below the overhang, to stop the rain dripping on passers-by.

It is thought that there are around 600 thatchers plying their trade in England, the better craftsmen being generally booked up for more than a year ahead. There are excellent future prospects for a young man entering the profession and a good living wage. There are supposedly 50,000 thatched dwellings in England, so there is always likely to be plenty of work.

Fire is one of the chief hazards. With modern fuel it is very rare for sparks to fly out of a chimney and ignite the roof, but if there is a fire inside the house, the thatch easily catches alight and can very quickly make an unpleasant conflagration. Insurance premiums are appreciably less for residences with non-combustible roofing material. For thatch the premiums are anything from three to five times the normal, in addition to which the insurance of the contents is increased in a similar proportion. Premiums vary widely and it probably pays to approach an organisation such as the County Gentlemen's Association who are sympathetic to thatch, than to go to one of the better-known insurance companies, most of whom are markedly shy about insuring it. There is a fire-retardent solution in which the thatching material may be soaked before use but this is not often done.

In medieval times fires in cities were a common occurrence and had a devastating effect as they swept through the houses with thatched roofs, the majority of which were of timber construction. As early as 1189 the first Lord Mayor of London, Henry Fitz-Alwin, decreed, 'No houses should be built in the city but of stone and then be covered with slate or burnt lime.' Houses with thatch had to plaster over roofs to minimise the risk.

Thatchers are their own masters, hardy, tough and independent with no two operating in exactly the same way. Their work can be recognised individually. Heavy snow or rain is about the only thing that holds them up. Even when the elements prevent thatching, the time can be usefully spent splitting hazel rods to make some of the many hundreds of spars needed, though some thatchers prefer to purchase these ready-made. Many operate alone, though it is more usual to have a mate, and some work in gangs. It is only the latter that can tackle the really big jobs such as churches, most of which are in Norfolk. Thatchers spend most of their working day on a ladder which is uncomfortable in itself, and they always wear heavy thick-soled footwear as well as knee pads either made out of leather by a saddler or cut out of an old car tyre. The transport of all their materials entails a good deal of going up and down ladders carrying big loads. The working position is never very comfortable as the body usually has to be twisted to one side, more often to the right as work generally proceeds from right to left with the ladders being moved around as required. As new work is very slippery, most thatchers have had a tumble. As a precaution the bottom of the ladder is always firmly secured, usually by a rope attached to an iron peg to prevent it slipping.

A thatcher normally assesses the cost by the number of squares of 100 square feet of roof and quotes accordingly. He has also to gauge with great accuracy the amount of material required. There must be enough for the job and not too much excess.

Normally a chimney has a lead flashing around it. On the upper side the lead extends up under the thatch which is cut off several inches away from the chimney in the form of a brow leaving a gulley for the rainwater. The flashings on the side usually extend

73

over the top of the thatch. Alternately a protruding fillet is fitted to throw rainwater out on to the thatch and give protection to the vulnerable joint where the thatch comes up against the chimney. Another weak point is any valley due to dormer windows or gables. An angled valley is liable to hold leaves and rubbish which accelerate the rotting of the thatch. For this reason valleys are usually swept either by building out the battens or packing the angle with a bolster of straw. This produces a very attractive finished effect with gentle curves. The ornamental finish is up to the craftsman but some like to have a bird such as a pheasant or peacock sitting on the roof. These are shaped out of straw that is bound with twine, sometimes painted and as a rule encased in a piece of wire netting.

The patterns of spars depends on the individual thatcher and can be a distinctive feature along the roof ridge and under dormer windows. These touches of individualism and art help to give a most pleasing finish to a neatly thatched dwelling.

If moss gets established on the roof it will speed up the deterioration. Overhanging trees are undesirable whilst birds can cause havoc though most thatch is wired over to prevent this. In the case of a roof thatched with Norfolk reed, sedge is used for the ridge and will probably need replacing two or three times before it becomes necessary to rethatch.

Long straw thatching has the shortest life, and might last for around fifteen years. Wheat reed is likely to have an expectancy of about twenty-five years and Norfolk reed about seventy-five. These figures are very approximate. Other factors are the skill of the craftsman, the quality of the thatching material and the geographical position of the house, an exposed position shortening its life. If damp penetrates at any weak spots and does not receive attention damage will occur to the battens, spars and twine.

Norfolk and Suffolk are the counties possessing most thatch and this is almost entirely of Norfolk reed, sometimes containing wild iris. Very occasionally one is composed entirely of sedge. Elsewhere thatch is to be found in all corn-growing districts—chiefly the

Midlands and South, where the method used is usually long straw thatching. In the West wheat reed predominates, particularly in Devon. However, now that most thatchers possess cars and can travel some way to work, any type of thatch can be seen anywhere.

The craft has been handed down from father to son or an apprentice and it is rather surprising that methods are so similar over wide areas. The nomenclature of tools varies slightly, for instance in the spelling of leggett which can also be written leggat. Some people talk about ledgers and others liggers. In recent years CoSIRA, the Council of Small Industries in Rural Areas, which has absorbed the Rural Industries Bureau, has produced a standard work on thatch called *The Thatcher's Craft* which gives details of the best ways to thatch, all very clearly shown by numerous photographs. They also run courses so that apprentices learn the best methods of achieving the highest standard.

NORFOLK REED

The reed is cut in winter when the long leaves have been stripped by frost. This means that cutting does not start till December and is carried on till the new growth begins to appear in April. Originally it was done by sickle or scythe but this process has now been partly mechanised. Generally it is cropped every year, though occasionally bi-annually, and achieves a height between 3 and 8 feet. Regular harvesting makes the reed grow straight and clean. The cut reed is then tied into bundles 12 inches in diameter, having first been sorted out into long, short and coarse grades.

A roof to be rethatched first has all the old covering stripped off to reveal the battens. Any woodwork requiring repair is made good. Then the reed is applied, with extra care at the start. Normally the work proceeds from right to left and is worked upwards in courses as opposed to lanes as in long straw thatching. To start off, a bunch of reed is placed on the wall plate with a foot or two of overhang, which will be trimmed later, and is secured to the battens with a length of tarred twine. If there is a gable end or barge this first bunch has to be laid at an angle of 30–40°, so that the butt ends of the reed stick outwards. As work proceeds along the eaves the bunches are tied on at a decreasing angle so after several feet they become vertical. The bunches are thicker at the bottom than the top and when tied become slightly concave so that on the finished roof little shows except the ends of the reed. Rain is thrown off by dripping off the ends rather than running down the reed.

The second course of reed is laid over the first, and hazel rods called sways, up to 8 feet in length and 1 inch in diameter, are laid over this. Thatching hooks some 10 inches long hold down the rod. The hooks which are shaped like a number 7 have a sharp point on the end and are hammered into the rafters underneath. Thus the work proceeds up the roof each succeeding course completely covering the sway holding the course below. The hazel

A Norfolk reed thatcher with his equipment. He is holding a leggett

sways are sometimes attacked by woodworm when they get old.
Should one of them break a section of the roof some 8 or 10 feet
in length will begin to slip and necessitate an awkward repair job.
To overcome this, some thatchers are trying out metal sways of
bright mild steel, but as with all new ideas the older hands are
wary and are unlikely to change until these have been proved. As
work proceeds the reed is beaten up tight by the use of a leggett.
This consists of a piece of wood measuring about 10 inches by 8
inches with a handle set at an angle. The face has flattened studs or
nails, some two dozen in number which project out about $\frac{1}{2}$ inch.
The ends of the reed are hit up tight under the sways and the roof
takes on a very neat and well-groomed appearance. Work proceeds
upwards till the ridge is reached and this calls for special treatment
as reed does not bend so cannot be laid over the top. It is therefore
trimmed with a large-bladed knife. Then a thick layer of sedge is
placed over the top of the ridge to form a skirt.

Sedge becomes dry and hard so before use it has to be well
wetted or, alternatively, used when it is still green. Over this sedge
runs a roll of reed neatly tied up and extending the whole length of
the ridge. Finally this roll is covered over with a further yealm of
sedge. The whole is then spicked down and the sedge skirt cut into
an attractive scalloped finish. The last operation is to go over the
whole roof again beating it up tight with the leggett and removing
any loose reed and sedge from the roof. Frequently there are
dormer windows and the reed round these has to be laid uniformly
to give a symmetrical finish and must project all round to throw off
the rain and will be trimmed with attractive-looking eyebrows.

Norfolk thatch is more expensive than other forms and costs
roughly 20 per cent more than wheat reed.

Obviously it appears most frequently in Norfolk where its use is
universal and includes such large areas as church roofs. The largest
expanse of thatch in the country is the Tithe Barn at Place Farm,
Tisbury in Wiltshire, which has an area of 1,450 square yards. This
was rethatched in Norfolk reed in 1971 by a team of five men who
took four months over the job. No less than 130,000 bundles of

A team of Norfolk reed thatchers putting a new roof-covering on the Tithe Barn at Tisbury, Wiltshire. It has the biggest area of thatch in the country: 1,450 square yards

reed were used with a total weight of approximately 270 tons. This barn, in common with most thatched churches had a good clean roof, uncomplicated by windows, though there were four gables over the barn doors. The thatch should last some seventy-five years, though it may need some maintenance from time to time.

When patching, some of the existing reed is partly pulled out, additional shorter reed pushed in, and it is all then beaten up tight with a leggett. Sedge does not last so long and will probably have to be renewed after twenty-five years. The Tisbury barn was finally covered with wire, though this is not usually done with reed, except possibly along the ridge and the eaves.

In future it seems likely that an increasing percentage of Norfolk reed thatch will be seen, providing the growers can supply enough as it lasts two or three times longer than other forms of thatch. Richer people are slowly displacing the poorer who previously lived under thatch, and being able to afford the extra few hundred pounds that it will cost, the more discerning of them will probably insist on reed.

COMBED WHEAT REED

A house thatched in combed wheat reed looks very like one of Norfolk reed and it requires a close and expert inspection to tell the difference. The finish of both is clean, close cropped, smooth and pleasing to the eye.

This type of thatch predominates in Devon and the west where it is usually called Devon reed.

There is little difference in the methods of thatching a roof in combed wheat and Norfolk reed. Those who thatch using the former method can usually work in Norfolk reed as well, though Norfolk reed thatchers rarely depart from their native material. One of the main differences is that reeded wheat straw is about 3 feet in length, about half that of Norfolk reed.

Before work starts, the bunches (which usually weigh 28 pounds) are butted, leaving the lower ends of the straw neat and level. These are divided into smaller handfuls for easy working and tied to the battens with tarred twine to form the first course. This has to be the most firmly secured as it is subjected to the stress of strong winds putting a strain on the underside of the eaves. Thereafter there are two methods of holding down the thatching straw.

In the first it may be held in place by sways secured by thatching hooks which are hammered into the roof rafters whose position has been located by probing with a thatching pin. Work then proceeds in courses in a similar way to Norfolk reed. Alternatively all the thatch may be tied on which is a slower but cheaper method as sways and thatching hooks can be dispensed with. For this method there have to be open rafters and an assistant working inside who removes the thread after it has been pushed through the straw with a thatching needle. This is then withdrawn and again pushed through in a new place and rethreaded from inside. When the needle is next withdrawn, the twine is pulled out enabling the thatcher to tie the wad on with a knot.

This method is used over the whole roof which finishes up about 18 inches thick and completely watertight. As work proceeds it is beaten up tight with a leggett and finally lightly trimmed using a shaving hook to give it the final smooth characteristic look.

The leggett for wheat reed differs from the Norfolk type. The latter has projecting nails whereas the former has a number of wooden grooves to force the straw up tight. In addition it is usual to have a second one with a hand grip on the back for use in awkward positions.

The ridge has an extra layer of straw sparred down over it and finally is given a pattern of cross spars to make an attractive finish. The spars used are about 2 feet in length, pointed at both ends which are deftly twisted and turned into a hairpin shape. The twist is important as it ensures that the fibres of the wood are not broken. The spar is then forced into the thatch and hammered tight with a mallet.

If well laid with good-quality straw, this type of roof should last around twenty-five years, but it is a wise precaution to have it over-hauled every three or four years in order to make good any weak points which are most likely to occur round chimneys or dormer windows.

As in Norfolk reed, the butt ends of the wheat are exposed and take most of the wear and tear.

LONG STRAW

Long straw thatching, although very pleasing, has a less smooth and sophisticated look than wheat reed, nor is it so durable, having a life expectancy of around fifteen years.

A close inspection shows it to be shaggy in appearance lying on a roof rather like the hair on a human head, the outer layer showing mostly the stem of the straw as opposed to the ends of it as in wheat reed.

There are variations in style and method when putting it on a roof. One way is to tie a layer of around 9 inches in thickness over the whole area using a tarred twine that is knotted to the battens except for the lower course which is probably secured by a rod or ledger held down by thatching hooks driven in to the wall plate, the piece of timber running along the top of the wall. Having completed the first layer, another one is secured over this of the same thickness giving the roof a final depth of 18 inches. The second layer is fixed to the first by laying rods or spars over the straw that are held down by spicks or spars twisted into a V-shape and forced in by a mallet or the palm of a reinforced glove. They are driven in with a slightly upward direction to discourage water finding its way into the thatch. All spars are covered over by each succeeding bundle of straw and do not show at all except just above the skirting and possibly on the rump or curve of a roof.

Long straw thatch is invariably finished in a decorative and attractive pattern with lines of parallel spars or rods about a foot apart with criss-cross spars. Wheat reed thatch does not normally have this embellishment so its presence indicates long straw thatching. The straw is supplied in yealms and is usually dampened and applied moist, having previously been manipulated to bring all the stems parallel. A length of stem of 3 feet is desirable.

The second layer is usually laid in lanes of about 30 inches in width and some thatchers prefer to finish as they go. The final operation is to brush down with a hand-rake which probably consists of nothing more than a length of wood with nails driven through. This removes any loose bits of straw. A pair of shears can be used to do any extra trimming. Having completed a lane, the thatcher then moves his ladder along to work the next one.

Most thatchers use a long one-piece ladder as opposed to an extending one, though sometimes a short ladder with hooks at the top is used for the awkward stretches.

The last operation is to trim around the barges and eaves with a sharp knife or hook which cuts through the straw quite easily giving it a very neat finish. Then all is covered over with wire netting of a mesh fine enough to keep out the birds. Though it is almost imperative to wire over long straw thatch, it has the disadvantage of trapping small leaves and moss and requires renewing from time to time. the frequency depending on the quality. A recent development is the use of a synthetic nylon type of netting which has the advantage of being inconspicuous and far easier to put on. This looks like being a successful idea, but has yet to stand the test of time and has to overcome the conservatism of the older type of craftsmen who tend to be suspicious of anything new.

Most of the thatcher's work consists of either patching or renewing an existing roof. Patching frequently leaves the tell-tale spars exposed here and there on the roof which detract from the appearance.

To rethatch it is first necessary to remove the top layer of existing straw by pulling it out. It may look old and discoloured on the outside, but within, the original gold colour will be preserved for years. All will be well if the rain has not penetrated through the thatch and rotted the battens which are nowadays probably made of softwood that has been treated with a preservative, whereas in bygone days they were of much more durable cleft oak. The new top coat of thatch is put on and held down by spars with the roof taking on a final thickness that may be slightly more than the original.

A single thatcher can use every year on average the straw from 40 acres of wheat, the exact amount depending on how much is new work and how much patching, the latter requiring more labour and less straw.

BUILDING MATERIALS

HAND-MADE BRICKS

BRICKS WERE made in this country as far back as Roman times. These were much thinner than the kind we know today and on account of this were well burnt and therefore durable. A number of examples are still to be seen mostly in churches, bricks which were removed from their original buildings and embodied in newer ones at a later date.

After the departure of the Romans very little brickmaking took place in England for the next thousand years.

In general, dwellings were constructed of the materials most readily and cheaply available, largely stone, sometimes flint and often timber.

During medieval times the only large buildings were those erected by the church or the castles of the barons, nobody else having the wealth to build on a grand scale.

After the suppression of the monastries by Henry VIII, there was a wider distribution of wealth and much more building took place.

Mansions, manor houses and colleges of learning sprang up everywhere. The demand for materials increased and brick began to be used on a greater scale, particularly in districts where there was no suitable stone.

Brick came into general use in the Netherlands before this country and most of the early brick was brought in as ballast in the returning wool ships. It was mostly used in East Anglia. Flemish craftsmen then came across and set up their kilns in this country.

If water transport was not available, bricks had to be made locally provided clay of the right consistency was obtainable.

The early bricks were burnt in wood-fired kilns, though from Elizabethan times onwards coal began to be used wherever possible. As time progressed they became cheaper and were transported throughout the network of canals and later by rail.

Local brickworks increased in importance and sprang up in all clay districts. Recently a few large concerns have begun to monopolise the industry using mechanisation and factory methods on a larger scale to produce bricks comparatively cheaply though of a monotonous similarity and colour. This has resulted in nearly all the smaller concerns being forced out of business and few handmade brickworks have survived.

Bricks are joined together by mortar, usually referred to as bonding. They are laid in a number of different ways. Much of the earlier work was done in 'English bond'. This entailed building one complete course, called the stretcher course, with the long narrow side of the brick facing outwards. The next course had only the ends exposed and is the header course. Rows continued upwards with alternate stretcher and header courses. 'Flemish bond' which was used extensively has alternate stretcher and headers in each course, but spaced so that the vertical joints of adjacent courses are never directly above one another as this could cause weakness.

There are other variants such as 'garden wall' but they are not as common.

In Tudor times it was very popular to have a pattern made by black bricks, these being the ones more fully burnt, usually in the form of diamonds and called diaper work. To this day one can often see dates or initials picked out in this manner prominently displayed to view.

In 1784 a tax was introduced on bricks by the thousand and in some cases oversized ones were made to lessen the tax which was eventually repealed in 1850.

Whatever the building material, chimneys were invariably lined with brick. In the case of timber-built houses, this was to obviate the risk of fire, and with stone houses, to prevent the stone being eroded away by the damaging effects of acid sulphur fumes given off by coal.

Cavity walls, which are now compulsory, began to be universally adopted about 1900 so that now all brickwork is built in stretcher bond, the outer skin being secured to the inner by metal ties.

To make a brick the first necessity is satisfactory clay. To obtain this the topsoil has to be removed and the clay dug out. It differs greatly in its chemical composition and this gives the finished article a varying colour around the country ranging from almost white or straw to shades of red sometimes tinged a bluish hue right through to black. Red colours are due to the presence of iron, straw to magnesia. Moreover there can be a colour variation in the burning of one batch of clay, with the higher temperatures creating a darker shade on the bricks nearer the source of heat.

Once dug, the clay is usually left to weather so that the rain can wash out some of the impurities. It was at one time a statutory obligation to leave it exposed during the winter. One can sometimes see bricks during freezing weather covered with a white efflorescence due to the presence of undesirable salts.

Before use the clay has to be pugged—a kneading process to mix it and at the same time break up lumps and remove impurities such as stones and shells. Originally this was done by treading with the bare feet. Later a horse-operated pug mill came into operation and finally it was power operated. Water is added as required to bring the clay to the necessary working condition and it is used within a few days of being pugged.

The hand brickmaker works at a bench upon which he places a few shovelfuls of the pugged clay. In front of him he has his mould which is a box of either metal or wood of a very exact size. This size varies with every brickworks as clays shrink different amounts and the final brick has to finish up with dimensions of approximately 9 by $4\frac{1}{2}$ by $2\frac{1}{4}$ inches. These measurements have been arrived at over a period of time and are the most convenient for the size of an average man's hand. The length is double the width which in turn is double the height, the former two measurements being important relative to one another when it comes to bonding.

The mould has no top or bottom but fits over a moulding stock on the bench which has a frog, and possibly the maker's name and initials. The frog gives a depression in the bottom of the completed brick to help the mortar adhere and give a stronger bond.

To start work the mould is placed over the stock, some sand thrown inside, a lump of clay is chopped off the pile, rolled in sand and then literally thrown into the mould with a strong downward movement. This has the effect of forcing the clay into the corners and edges and filling it completely and perfectly. A piece of wire usually strung across a bow of wood is run over the top of the mould and the surplus clay is removed. The mould then has a wooden pallet put over it and with a quick turn the clay in the shape of a brick is turned out on to it and placed on a long, flat, bearing-off barrow which carries one layer of bricks. They are then wheeled off to be dried under cover, being carefully stacked so that air can circulate freely around them. This is a slow process during which the brick must not be subjected to any draughts, frost, rain or sunshine that might dry it unevenly. The brick begins to shrink as it dries and might warp very slightly causing a small amount of loss at this stage. Some small concerns only moulded bricks in the summer so that when winter came along the clay had dried out sufficiently to be able to withstand any frosts without disintegrating. This routine meant that more labour was required in the summer for pugging, moulding and storing the bricks whilst in the winter the firing took place and less was needed. The

86

surplus men probably went off to cut the woodland coppices in the winter.

It is amazing the speed at which a brickmaker can work and the number of bricks that can be moulded in a day. The work entails moving a heavy weight of clay and the craftsmen needs to be very fit, possibly more so than for any other craft.

Whilst the moulding of bricks is not all that difficult, the stacking and firing of the kiln calls for a high degree of skill and experience as the whole kilnful can be ruined in this stage. It is all done by eye. In the past the kiln operator preferred to be on his own during the firing and took good care not to teach anybody else his job. In this way, he became indispensable and his employment assured for as long as bricks were needed.

Originally clamps were used for the final state of burning the clay. These were built after the manner of a charcoal burner's clamp finishing up in the shape of a mound. This type was superseded by the kiln, a rectangular building probably with an open top and fire holes in the two long sides. At the ends are the doorways allowing entrance for the barrow loads of bricks. The barrows are of a characteristic design so that when loaded with sixty bricks and with the handles raised the balance of the load comes directly over the wheel, pneumatic tyred these days, enabling a heavy load to be carried with comparative ease. One type of kiln has an end built up so that half the kiln is loaded from one entrance and the other, and higher, end is used for loading the upper half. The bricks are laid with spaces between each one to enable the hot air to pass through freely. When loaded, some old bricks are placed closely over the top layer in the kiln to retain the heat. Finally the entrances are sealed with bricks and clay. The whole of the bonding of the kiln is of clay, as mortar would disintegrate in the heat.

Then the fires are started. There might be four on each side of the kiln which could be holding 40,000 bricks. At first the heat has to be applied very slowly. There is still a certain amount of moisture in the bricks and too fierce a heat might turn this to steam and cause them to crumble. White smoke is given off as the contents are slowly dried out for two or three days and then the fires are stoked up to a much fiercer heat causing a blue shimmering haze over the kiln and the bricks to glow red at night. This temperature has to be very carefully regulated for two crucial days with wind or rain adding to the difficulties. When the brickmaker judges that sufficient burning has taken place the furnace holes are blocked up with brick and clay and the kiln allowed to cool slowly for a week or so before unloading. The completed bricks will vary in colour and hardness depending on their position in the kiln. Those further down become harder and darker in colour till at the bottom the ends of those nearest the fire may be quite black. If the process is carried too far, they may become glazed or melted, since a main constituent of clay is silica, from which glass is largely made. The finished bricks are sorted out into piles of various colours.

The addition of sand during the moulding process gives an attractive and slightly rough texture whilst the variation of heat in the kiln ensures a range of subtle colours far pleasanter than the depressing uniformity of the mass-produced articles. Moreover they will be very slightly less perfect in shape. Their properties give a finished house a distinguished look and add to the value to a greater extent than the additional cost. Discerning customers ensure a constant demand for hand-made bricks.

STONE

From Norman times onwards churches, castles and larger buildings were built of stone whenever it was available. The ease with which different types can be worked varies enormously and allowance has to be made for the fact that the quality and properties of even a particular kind of stone differ in each locality. Its character frequently depends upon the depth at which it is found. Some types of stone are very difficult to split; others, called freestone, can be sawn to give a smooth ashlar appearance.

The easiest way of obtaining stone is by quarrying. Mining necessitates burrowing underground, a more expensive and complicated way of procuring it but a practice carried out by the Romans to obtain their supplies of Bath stone.

Labour in those days was of little account in assessing the cost and stone was frequently easier to obtain than bricks which had to be made in wood kilns right up to medieval times and afterwards in many districts until the coming of coal.

The wearing qualities of different stones vary. Bath stone does not do well in London, being unable to stand up to the smoky acid atmosphere. Limestone from Portland, not so very different in texture, is far more satisfactory there. In general the sulphur-laden soot and smoke from coal fires erodes stone. Chimneys, therefore, are invariably lined with brick with a cast-iron backing plate behind the fire.

The colour of stone depends on the district and the chemical impurities. For instance the presence of iron stains the stone a reddish brown. Stone can be white, brown, or tinged with pink, to name but some of the shades.

With few exceptions stone must be laid in its bedding plane, that is the position in which it lays in the quarry. If this is done it will weather correctly and have a longer life. The exceptions are for such pieces that are made for balusters and coping-stones which should be laid with the bedding plane vertical.

Over the years many quarries have been closed owing to lack of demand and relatively high cost or else working out. Some small ones were opened especially for building great houses in Elizabethan times. The stone originally used for building the Houses of Parliament is no longer obtainable and a substitute has had to be used for repairs, some like the Headington stone that is employed so extensively at Oxford deteriorates rapidly after about 200 years.

Some stone such as granite and Purbeck marble takes a polish. The former can be used as a facing material for a building but the latter, which is not a true marble, is only suitable for inside work as it weathers badly.

Whatever the stone, in time it is eroded away by the elements particularly when exposed to the prevailing wind. The fine carvings on churches and university colleges need renewing sooner or later. Restoration work that is carried out is usually of a very fine quality —an indication that there are still masons with great skill though their numbers are not very large.

Unsurpassed as a building stone is the jurassic limestone which is to be found in a belt that includes the Portland and Bath areas extending up through the Midlands to Yorkshire. It is still quarried in several areas, chief of which is Portland. First the top soil and overburden have to be removed. The top layer of stone is generally unsuitable for building but can usefully be burnt for lime or used as roadstone. Under this will be found the good material which can be split up into pieces weighing up to 6 or 7 tons. Holes are made with pneumatic hammers around the side and end of the stone. A long-handled lever is then inserted in a suitable place in the bedding plane and forced down so that the block of stone splits off. The depth of the block can be up to 30 inches, the width about 3 feet and the length 6 feet. This can be handled by crane and is a suitable size for cutting. Every block is tapped for soundness with a piece of metal or a lump of stone. It should emit a clear ringing note if sound and a dull thud if cracked, the difference in tone being easily detected by the experienced man.

The mining of stone is a much more ambitious process and not very much is done now. It is still carried out near Bath to extract the famous stone that bears its name. Here the cutting is done by a machine similar to that used in the coal mines. It consists of a chain saw on an extending arm. Skill and experience are needed to know where to cut because of faults and cracks in the stone and also the fact that about a third of the material has to be left in the form of large pillars to support the strata that form the roof. Stone mined in this way contains about 10 per cent of moisture in the form of quarry sap which has to dry out. During the winter months it has to be stored below ground because, if exposed to frost, pieces would split off and the stone become powdery causing unnecessary wastage. The stone hardens as it dries with a crust forming on the outside.

Hand splitting a piece of limestone. First holes are made in the block, then it is split with wedges

From the mines and quarries the stone is sent away for cutting after it has been roughly squared and trimmed to shape with an axe to avoid transporting waste. In any case about 30 per cent is lost in the cutting process in which it is reduced to manageable-sized pieces. This can be done with a carborundum or a diamond-cutting wheel or even a hand-saw. The final size and shape depends on the requirements. Facing stones for buildings are usually 4 inches thick—about the minimum practical size.

As much masonry as possible is finished off at the works. Pieces like balusters are turned on a lathe whilst carving and copying are done by very skilled, but usually anonymous banker masons who take a great pride in their craft.

Experience and knowledge are needed to fix stonework. It is continually moving and absorbing moisture so great care has to be taken with the jointing. It must be less strong than the stone itself or pieces will chip off. Where cramps are used they should be of some metal like phosphor bronze or copper that does not rust. Iron is fatal as sooner or later it rusts, splitting the stone and doing immense harm. It is possible to use it by sheathing it in a lead covering. This was the practice in medieval times and is to be found in many churches.

Stonemasons exist in small numbers wherever there are quarries, but few of them are young. Monumental masons are kept busy lettering grave headstones, but the carved and symbolic ornamentation which was such a feature in the last century is rarely seen today. The stones are more functional, requiring no flair on the part of the mason.

There will always be a need for carved work, particularly for restoration, and consequently a steady demand for masons. The work requires both skill and patience and some of the art schools might produce masons of the necessary calibre.

STONE ROOFS

Stone roofs are to be found in a great many parts of the country particularly in the limestone belt that runs from Dorset right up to Yorkshire. They are also met within sandstone areas.

In some instances the material can be quarried and in others mined in shallow workings. However very little is produced nowadays owing to the expense and lack of demand.

In the areas where the stone roofing tiles were produced they were at one time both cheap and plentiful, and rich and poor alike used them. They provide an attractive roof material which is both long lasting and fire-proof and looks very well capping buildings made of the local stone.

Only certain stone is satisfactory for splitting; some will not split at all. In the places where there was a fissile type of stone the method was to quarry or mine it in the autumn and bring it to the surface. In this condition it has about 10 per cent of quarry sap or moisture content. When the hard frosts arrived they split the stone naturally. The moisture in the stone tended to dry out and so it was a common practice to pour water over it to keep it moist to aid the splitting. When the stone had dried out in the spring it became much harder and did not continue to flake. A certain amount of assistance in splitting was necessary after the frost action.

Stones for roofing are first sorted into different sizes usually after a hole has been made in the top by a small pick or a power drill. The bottoms of the tiles have to be square and are trimmed to shape with a hammer. The size is then measured from the bottom up to the hole made near the top. There is no limit to the width of the tile. It can be as wide as 30 inches and the height can be anything from about 6 inches to 30 inches, a variety of sizes being needed as roofs are invariably laid with courses of a diminishing size as the ridge is approached. The thickness of individual tiles also varies slightly.

Stone tiles can last almost for ever, unless broken by falling off a roof.

Though practically no new ones are produced there is luckily still a small source of supply from the roofs of derelict farm buildings. Stone roofs are very heavy indeed and on nearly all old buildings the roof line becomes uneven under the strain of the weight over a period of years. When stone roofs give trouble the cause is nearly always due to the entry of rain. The woodwork rots and the tiles begin to slip off and fall, accelerating the damage unless quickly attended to.

Stone tiles are hung on the battens, not nailed, their weight being sufficiently heavy to prevent the wind blowing them off. Sometimes oak pegs are used for hanging and these will last for easily 100 years if kept dry. Iron nails are frequently used but are attacked by rust. Copper or aluminium give more satisfactory results and last almost indefinitely. Apart from moisture, damage might be caused by the depredations of woodworm attacking the battens.

In places like barns and farm outbuildings, whose roofs are usually unlined, it is possible to see how the tiles are hung, but houses invariably have a lining usually of wood with a layer of felt over it.

Another feature of a stone roof is the steep pitch that is very necessary as stone tiles, unlike slates, tend to be somewhat uneven in thickness and a strong wind could blow rain up and under a shallow pitch. The minimum requirement is to have a slope of at least 45° though a greater slope means that more tiles are needed so making the roof very much heavier.

On old roofs the spaces between the battens usually had some form of infilling. In medieval times it was often dry moss and later mortar, probably over a layer of felt made of hair.

Nowadays there is usually a layer of roofing felt or some synthetic material between the lining and the battens.

It is not very common for a new house to have a stone roof though there is now on the market an artificial Cotswold roofing tile that looks very realistic and lies flatter.

Most of the roofing work today consists of repairs. They might mean stripping off the whole area and starting from scratch. In the process some stones are bound to become damaged so a number of spares of different sizes are needed. Having stripped a roof and lined it, the battens have to be nailed on. They are usually pieces of wood 2 inches by 1 inch, preferably treated with a preservative against fungus growth and woodworm. As the roof is almost certain to have diminishing-sized courses the battens become progressively close as the work proceeds upwards. They are usually nailed on one row at a time depending on the size of the tiles which govern their distance apart.

First the bottom row is laid but does not have the slates with the longest length. The second row has these because they are hung on a higher batten and exactly cover the whole of the bottom row which does not show at all. Any width stones can be used, though for preference the wider the better as there are less vertical joints and therefore the rain is kept out more effectively. Great care must be taken that the vertical joints of successive courses are staggered as, if they are in line, the roof would not be watertight.

(Opposite) On a stone roof, cement is only used to secure the ridge tiles and possibly to prevent tiles from rocking

In a finished roof only about 40 per cent of any tile is exposed. As the work approaches the top, the tiles become smaller and the work slower and more intricate. Care has to be taken that none of the slates rock because any movement caused by the wind eventually causes wear. Rocking can be prevented by using a small amount of mortar under the tile and out of sight.

The roof ridge calls for some special treatment. The usual method is to have the capping stones cut into a shape from a block of freestone which overlaps the top tiles and is cemented in place. The stones at the end of the roof or gable might have a more elaborate or carved finial.

The biggest area of stone roofs are probably on churches and one of average size might well have 10,000 tiles, need a hundredweight of nails to hang them and take six months to complete the work.

Reroofing is an expensive and inevitably rather slow job as every tile has its individual idiosyncrasy and the craftsman needs a keen eye to place them correctly and efficiently. The men usually write their signature and the date somewhere under the felt so that it will be seen in years to come when major repairs are carried out.

It is quite normal for a roof to last for 100 years and possibly double that time. Odd tiles might flake a little and may need renewing. As they are hung they can be replaced without much difficulty and a new one can be trimmed to the right dimensions to make a good fit.

Not enough roofs require repair for the work to offer a full-time job, so roof layers are versatile men usually practising some other craft in the building trade as well.

CORNISH SLATES

Slate has been a roofing material for many hundreds of years though until the coming of canals and railways its use was restricted to areas where it could be transported by sea or was available locally.

Slates are produced in Cornwall, Wales and Cumberland though in a greatly reduced volume now owing to production expense. The colours vary from slate grey, blue to grey-green, the latter coming from Cornwall and almost all from the Delabole slate quarry.

The great advantage of roofing slates is the fact they can be split into thin wafers that lie very flat on a roof enabling the structure to be built with comparatively light supporting rafters and a shallow pitch—both of which save costs. In addition they are hard and durable, lasting for centuries.

Georgian architects exploited these qualities by building very flat roofs that were behind parapets and for the most part hidden from view. Locally in Cornwall they afforded a first-class roofing material besides being frequently hung on the weather side of houses as a protection against the driving rain.

They are produced in a variety of standard sizes and thicknesses

Splitting Cornish roofing slates with a chisel and beetle

and as a rule are laid in diminishing-sized courses becoming progressively smaller towards the ridge of the roof.

To lay slates, two holes are made either by drilling or with a pointed pick about an inch from the long sides of the slate just above the half-way mark. Special large-headed galvanised nails are driven through these holes on to the roof batten starting at the bottom row and working upwards though it may proceed diagonally if all the slates are the same size. The subsequent slates are laid so they cover the nail holes leaving only about 40 per cent of their area exposed. Old roofs were usually secured with iron nails that rust in time causing slates to slide out. This in turn lets water into the roof, rots the battens and eventually major repairs have to be carried out. Should a single slate slip out a degree of dexterity is needed to refix or replace it as it is impossible to nail it back without stripping off a large area. The difficulty can be overcome by nailing a piece of wire or a strip of lead to the batten between the adjoining slates, replacing the slate and bending the wire or lead up under the lower edge to hold it in position.

When slates are hung on side walls, lime mortar is frequently used to keep them rigidly fixed and prevent rocking.

Probably the most attractive of all slates are those that come from the Delabole quarry in north Cornwall. A vast crater has been formed 40 acres in extent at the top. Five hundred feet below where it is being worked today the area is 10 acres. It is thought that this particular quarry was first worked over 600 years ago.

The slate is obtained by a mixture of drilling and blasting to procure 100 tons a day, a significant amount but minute compared with the 2,000 tons that were quarried daily 50 years ago. Of the 100 tons quarried only about 20 is good enough for making roofing slates and with wastage this is further reduced to approximately 5 tons. A huge amount of waste used to get piled up though nowadays it is all gainfully used by being crushed into roadstone. The raw material is cut to a manageable size by a circular saw with diamond cutters from whence it is passed to the men who split it and shape it to size.

These craftsmen sit on very low chairs with their legs stretched out in front of them. Taking a thick slab of slate they put it against a pad on the left leg and carefully place a broad chisel along the edge to be cut. The chisel head is struck with a wooden mallet called a beetle and after several blows the slate begins to split. It is then turned through 90° and the splitting process continues until a layer flakes off. The thickness varies with the quality of the slate, the heavier ones weighing double that of the lightest.

The next operation is to turn the split slate to the required size by holding the edge against a machine with a guillotine blade that comes down and snaps the edge leaving it with a straight side roughly bevelled.

The finished slates are finally graded into various sizes and thicknesses.

Taking into account the wastage and the fact that not many operations can be mechanised the final price of slate cannot be cheap so that one measuring 24 inches by 12 inches costs about 30p, making it a comparatively expensive form of roof covering.

This has resulted in the present-day demand being rather small and the one-time large work force being diminished to only a few men. Most slates are produced to meet specific orders.

CHAPTER 7

STONE WALLS

DRY STONE WALLS

DRY STONE walls are so called because no cement or mortar is used in their construction; they remain intact due to the skilful work of the craftsmen who make them. They are to be found in all districts where stone is plentiful and readily obtainable either by picking them off a field, from quarries or derelict walls. They may be built equally well of sandstone, limestone or slate.

Some that mark boundaries may be very old, but the majority have been made to partition the land after enclosure from the eighteenth century onwards. Wherever they are to be seen the principles of making them are the same though details and dimensions vary.

A spit of topsoil is first removed and some large foundation stones are laid giving a base about 3 feet thick and possibly two

(Opposite) Making a Cotswold dry stone wall. In the left foreground can be seen the template and the strings that control the dimensions

stones wide, any gap in the middle being filled with smaller pieces of stone or chippings. It is usual to use a template consisting of a wooden frame of the dimensions required for the finished wall which always slopes in towards the top giving it a batter. String lines are run from a template to a similar one placed some yards away so that the wall can be built to a uniform cross-section. Stones are carefully selected by shape and size to construct the wall which may be roughly built up in courses. The required number of stones are spread out along the length of wall being constructed, bearing in mind that all the surplus will need labour to remove it. Throughout the wall at regular intervals are the through or tie stones that play an essential part in holding it together. The builder has to select his stones very carefully by eye so they can be used to the best advantage. It is desirable that they slope slightly downwards to shed rainwater which means that their tails have to be pinned to stop them falling out. Larger stones are used lower down and smaller ones as the wall gains height until the top of the wall may only have a thickness of one stone. Along the very top, laid on edges, are the capping stones.

Apart from the template very few tools are required, possibly only a hammer or slater's axe to do a little rough trimming.

A well-laid wall will last a great many years providing it is reasonably maintained. Vandals can easily damage them and so can trees if allowed to grow close by. Ice is one of the chief enemies as it can loosen the stones.

Sometimes the tops of the walls and capping are mortared which may save some maintenance, though it looks a rather sorry sight if any of the stones below slip out, and it complicates the task of rebuilding.

Constructing dry walls is slow and expensive; a single man might be able to progress at a yard an hour. Most councils have men who can build them so that whenever a road is diverted a new wall is built to keep in harmony with the existing pattern.

Farmers view them with mixed feelings. They can cost a lot to repair but more important is the fact that with present-day expensive and sophisticated machinery larger fields are required and walls must go in spite of the labour needed to remove them.

Other aspects of stone walls are that they do not rob the soil like hedges with large trees, but they are rather soulless and give no sanctuary to birds. Being built of local stone they always harmonise with the surroundings and can be an attractive feature of their particular locality.

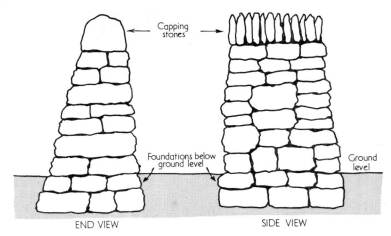

Dry stone walling

To be effective they have to be comparatively high, particularly to keep in rams who have great agility and climbing capacity and will take advantage of any defects.

DEVON WALLS

These are of a different construction to the dry stone walls. In essence they are a solid sandwich of large stones with earth between and a turf top. Trees grow quite readily in their tops and bind them together rather than force them apart. They stand up to the elements excellently, some being of great antiquity.

CHAPTER 8

MILLING

WATERMILLS

WATERMILLS WERE probably brought to Britain as long ago as Roman times and certainly the Saxons used them in increasing numbers so that at the time of the Domesday survey no less than 5,624 were recorded. These were virtually all watermills though it is possible a very few were powered by horses; windmills were a later development. The alternative to grinding corn by water power was the hand quern consisting of a fixed stone with a con-cave-shaped depression into which fitted the revolving stone that was turned by hand, this being a woman's or slave's job. The coming of the water-powered mills greatly speeded up the process of milling. The fact that they were driven by water meant that they had to be situated in places where a sufficient head of water could be obtained in order to drive the wheel. In addition there had to be enough population and sufficient corn available nearby to make it an economical proposition. The mills were owned almost entirely by the lords of the manor, the only people wealthy enough to be able to build them. All the peasants' corn had to be milled there, the 'soke' rights compelling everybody to do this, even if they wished to grind their own corn in hand querns. The miller took a percentage of the corn in payment.

Depending on the whereabouts of the water, the mill might be situated some way off and inconvenient for the local peasantry.

It was essential to have an adequate supply of water all the year round and the rights were jealously guarded with incessant litigation about their control and ownership.

Many mills were situated near a weir to give them their head of water. The construction of a weir was a big undertaking and usually a hindrance to navigation. Water transport was most important in medieval times as roads were so bad and a good deal of high feeling was caused by any new weir. The difficulty could sometimes be partially overcome by the building of a flash lock, a type with one gate through which a barge might pass, but inevitably the miller lost some of his precious water every time it was used.

Other methods of obtaining water were to have a mill-pond that was supplied by a stream which filled it up at night, ready for the miller to use by day. Alternatively the water might be channelled off from a river in a mill flume or leat controlled by hatches. Some of these artificial waterways are quite long and a miller looked after his rights tenaciously—the supply of water determined whether or not he remained in business.

Probably the most important part of a mill is the wheel. The very

Waterwheels

primitive ones were horizontal but of the remaining types to be seen all are fitted vertically. There are various kinds of wheel; the least efficient is the undershot which consists of a paddle wheel that is revolved by the velocity of the stream.

In a breast-shot wheel the water is fed into the wheel half-way up, usually filling compartments with water whose weight turns it. Lastly there is the overshot where water is fed in by a chute above the wheel filling the buckets and giving a high degree of efficiency of somewhat over 60 per cent or nearly three times that of the undershot type. An overshot wheel is used wherever there is a sufficient head of water available in such places as hilly country with fast-flowing streams. The larger the diameter of wheel the greater the power though there is a limit to the amount needed.

All the earliest wheels were of wood with elm playing a leading part as it does not mind being wet. In the eighteenth century cast-iron wheels began to be made and they eventually superseded wooden ones. They were generally constructed in a number of sections that could be bolted together on the site.

The water supply to the wheel was controlled by sluices and the water was carefully conserved and shut off when the mill was not working or when there was no load. In the latter case the wheel increased speed rapidly if care was not taken. A variant in an overshot is the pitch-back wheel. The supply chute is fitted so that the wheel revolves in the same direction as the tail-race water.

WINDMILLS

Windmills came after watermills and are first recorded in England in the twelfth century. They are usually located in cereal-growing districts where there are insufficient streams to provide power for a watermill or in flat country such as in East Anglia. In this area most of them are for pumping water to keep the land drained.

The oldest windmills are the post type in which a very large post, almost always of oak, is rigidly fixed and on which the whole body or buck of the mill revolves. The best in the world were those of East Anglia, of which Saxted Green is a splendid example of one that has been fully restored.

At a later stage the windmill with a revolving cap was invented. The advantage of this type is that the body can remain stationary, leading in turn to the smock mill, which is usually an octagonal wooden building frequently built on a stone or brick base. This variety of mill tapers slightly towards the top which is surmounted by the cap.

Finally came the tower mill constructed of brick with thick walls at the base gradually becoming thinner towards the top. These rise to a great height with as many as five separate floors in the biggest examples.

A century ago there were 10,000 windmills in operation but with the arrival of steam power they gradually fell into disuse until today only about 100 are preserved, with but a mere handful working commercially. Some have become houses, others are restored and working occasionally for demonstrations and public viewing.

The body of a mill is frequently older than the internal machinery which may have been renewed at a later date.

The oldest preserved windmills are 300 years of age and are of the post variety. Often they are a type called open-trestle post mills in which the post with supporting quarter bars mounted on cross trees resting on brick pillars are all visible underneath the main

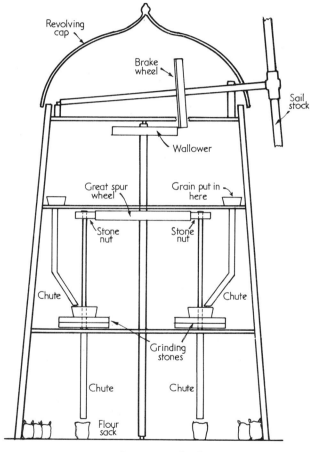

A tower windmill

108

The base of an open-trestle windmill at Bourne, Cambridge

body. Frequently all of this is enclosed in a circular building called a round house which acts as a store and working-space around the base of the mill.

A post mill is constructed entirely of wood having many large baulks of oak which were usually cut and shaped when the wood was still green and unseasoned.

Protruding out of the back of a post mill is a huge tail pole used for revolving the complete structure in order to manoeuvre the sails to face the wind for operating the mill. The miller has to be constantly on the lookout for a change of wind and has to turn his windmill whenever this happens. To help in this operation the tail pole is often fitted with a cart-wheel and later examples have a fan-tail which does the turning automatically. There is also a long ladder for the miller to enter the mill.

The fan-tail has revolving vanes driving through cogged gearing to keep the windmill facing the direction of the wind.

The invention of the fan-tail led to the development of the smock and tower mills in which the body remains still and a cap on top revolves. The cap carries the sails in the front and fan-tail at the back.

Most windmills have four sails though the number varies up to a maximum of eight.

The sails have several variations: canvas spread out on a wooden frame; those with wooden louvres operated by springs for regulating their spread; and finally patent sails which opened louvres by a series of fulcrums operated from inside the mill, so giving the miller an easier time. Eventually their adjustment became automatic and could be set by varying weights.

With canvas sails the speed is regulated by the amount of canvas set. This is adjusted by reefing that can only be done after stopping the sails revolving by applying the brake. The brake consists of a

A smock mill that towers over Cranbrook in Kent

very large wheel mounted on the windshaft, to which the sails are attached, with a band of wood or metal round its circumference. A lever applies pressure to the band and the friction makes it stop, at the same time generating a good deal of heat so that care has to be taken to avoid a fire.

The cap revolves on a circular kerb around the circumference of the top of the mill which has to be dead level and true.

In the earliest mills there was a wood to wood surface which was kept well greased. In later ones the cap has bearings or wheels running on a concrete kerb.

The windshaft has the sails attached to it one end with a fitting such as a canister to which the sail stocks are bolted or wedged in. A striking bar passing through the centre of the windshaft enables patent sails to be operated from inside the mill whilst the sails still revolve.

The sails themselves are wider at the extremities and are built with a slight twist embodying the characteristic that later went into the construction of aeroplane propellors.

A windmill is designed to face into the wind and one of the great dangers is being caught with a strong gust coming from behind, technically known as being 'tail winded'. Millers dread this happening as it puts a great strain on the structure and in extreme cases has lifted off the whole cap and even blown down some old post mills.

The caps varied in shape and construction and gave each mill an individual appearance ranging from the attractive ogee to the dome-shaped. The outside colouring of a mill varies. Many have white-painted bodies; others have a protective coating of tar which is probably more serviceable but has a rather sombre look.

In larger tower and smock mills there is usually a gallery some way up which goes all round the outside of the mill for the purpose of tending the sails. As a rule a round house circles the base for storage of both flour and grain.

THE MACHINERY

Windmills and watermills have most of the internal machinery in common. In a windmill the sails rotate the windshaft to which is attached the brake wheel. This drives the wallower on the centre line attached to a vertical driving shaft. In a watermill the waterwheel shaft has a pit wheel attached that drives the wallower which in turn is keyed to the driving shaft.

In both types of mill the great spur wheel is attached to the

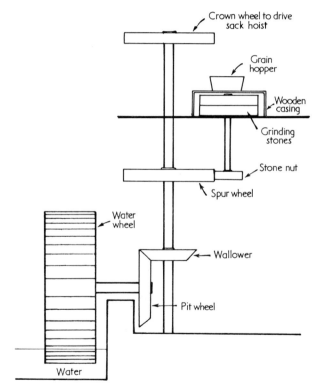

Watermill machinery

driving shaft and drives the stone nuts. A shaft passes through these and rotates the stones.

The stones themselves are in pairs and usually of either millstone grit from Derbyshire or French burr. The latter are made up of about a dozen separate pieces mounted in plaster of Paris or cement and bound together with an iron band round the circumference. Occasionally one comes across a composite stone or those from the Cologne area. They vary in size but are mostly 4 feet in diameter and weigh about a ton. Transporting them was a considerable problem on the poor roads. They were taken as far as possible by water and then put on their sides, a shaft was run through the hole in the centre and a horse pulled them along.

In early mills all the machinery was made of wood. The revolving wheels had mortice holes to take the cogs which were usually made of hornbeam or apple for strength. With the coming of cast iron in the mid-eighteenth century, progressively less wood was used.

The various shafts were made of metal and so were some of the cogged wheels, though many wheels were fitted with wooden cogs, a combination of wood and iron giving a quiet and satisfactory drive. In the event of an accident a few wooden cogs would shear and could be replaced without too much difficulty. There were invariably an odd number of cogs fitted in order that they always meshed differently ensuring more even wear.

The stones could be driven either from above or below, the practice differing with the individual mill. The direction of drive could also vary, but was more frequently clockwise.

The stone nuts can usually be raised to engage or disengage the stones or alternatively a few cogs are removed to disengage them. The speed of the drive is important and depends on the size of the stones. With a 4-foot-diameter stone a speed of around 120 revolutions a minute is a good average. This is achieved by gearing depending on the size of wheels and number of cogs. In turn in a watermill the wheel speed is controlled by the sluice and in a windmill by the speed of rotation of the sails depending on the amount of canvas set, the tension of the spring on patent sails and the wind velocity. As the latter varied the miller had a more difficult task in a windmill.

The stones are always in pairs. The lower or bed stone remains stationary and has to be absolutely level. The upper stone is the runner and is dressed to be very slightly concave. The stones should never touch each other but ought to be set apart about the thickness of a sheet of paper. Should they inadvertently touch they wear very quickly as well as generate a lot of heat with the risk of fire, a fate which befell a number of mills in the past.

When the stones gather speed and warm up, the gap between them increases and makes coarse or improperly ground flour if left unadjusted. To take care of this there is a clever piece of mechanism, called the tentering gear. This enables the gap to be adjusted manually or by a governor which automatically alters with the speed of rotation of the runner stone.

Needless to say everything has to be most carefully balanced in order to avoid any vibrations, a more intricate achievement in the case of a post mill in which the whole body revolves.

The number of pairs of wheels varies from a single pair in the older and more primitive mills to two or three pairs for the majority of others. These are usually of different types as each kind has its own characteristics and grinding properties.

The miller himself is usually a handyman and can carry out minor running repairs but a professional millwright is needed for the bigger jobs.

DRESSING THE STONES

Everything in a mill has to be perfectly balanced and smooth running but the ultimate success of the end-product largely depends on the millstones and how they are dressed, a term used to describe how the pattern of grooves is cut and kept in condition. This is the job of the expert and was usually done by men who travelled round doing nothing else.

This can also be done by most millers but it detracts from their other work and is a very specialised art. Nowadays the miller him-self has to do it, as the itinerant craftsmen have all disappeared due to insufficient work.

The grooves for the stones must have a cutting edge to shear the cereal with a scissor-like action as the top wheel revolves and then to grind it into a very fine powder for the end product.

To dress the stones the runner, which is the top one, has to be removed either by hoisting it with a lifting gibbet or purchase or merely turning it over with wooden levers. The stone is then left supported on sacks, the grooved surfaces of both stones being now left exposed ready for operations to start. The manhandling of the runner stones takes two or three men.

The bed stone is first carefully trued up with any high spots being reduced until it is absolutely level and found to be so by the use of a long, narrow, cast-iron 'proof stall'. Then work may begin on the grooves. The pattern is the same for both stones which are usually divided into harps or segments with a master furrow which runs at a slight tangent to the eye at the centre of the wheel. The furrows are a little more than an inch wide being very shallow near the centre and about $\frac{1}{2}$ inch deep or slightly more at the circumference. Each segment has four furrows. The level parts of the stone be-tween the furrows are called lands, on which there are very fine grooves, called 'stitching' or 'cracking'.

The millwright has a specialised set of tools to carry out this work. Most important is his thrift, a wooden-handled implement into which fit the mill bills. These are sharply pointed at each end and are made of carbon steel very carefully tempered. The grooves are recut by rapid pecking with these bills, which need replacing for sharpening every twenty minutes or so in addition to re-tempering from time to time.

The top stone is usually made slightly concave with very little clearance near the centre but gradually increasing to about $\frac{1}{2}$ inch at the edge.

The frequency of dressing depends on the type of stone and the amount of running that it has done and a fair average is about a

The inside of a working mill showing the casings around the stones and the food hoppers above them

month between dressings with each pair taking a day or more to dress.

With use a stone gradually wears thinner. A peak stone of Derbyshire millstone grit starts with a thickness of 16 inches and can be used until it gets down to 3 inches after which it is relegated to a garden ornament or otherwise disposed of.

There are other patterns, such as spirals, for stone dressing but these are not so common. There is no fixed way for the runner stone to turn, in some mills they rotate clockwise and in others anti-clockwise.

GRINDING THE CORN

For grinding the first operation is to get the sacks of grain to the upper floor of the mill. This is done by a sack hoist using a power take-off from the main shaft. It is often said that a miller never has to do any manual work as his machinery does it all for him.

It greatly facilitates the miller's work to have a helper to do such tasks as tying the sacks on to the hoisting gear. The sacks pass up through trapdoors fitted with leather hinges which drop shut when they have passed up and on reaching the top floor the contents are emptied into a bin. From here the grain feeds down into a wooden hopper just above the stones and trickles out into the feed shoe which is kept continually joggled by the damsel, so named because it continually chatters.

The grain slowly feeds through the eye of the runner stone and is then sheared and ground between the two stones gradually being forced outwards by centrifugal force. On reaching the edge of the stone it falls between the bed stone and the casing eventually finding its way down a chute into a bin or sack, having become quite hot in the process.

The miller keeps a constant eye on the fineness of the flour by periodically feeling a sample between the thumb and forefinger which in time gives him a flattened 'miller's thumb'.

Wheat for flour is usually ground by French burr stones which are harder, whilst the slightly softer Derbyshire millstones are used for grinding barley in the production of grist for cattle. A pair of 4-foot stones can grind around 5 bushels an hour or about 300 pounds.

After grinding, the wheatmeal is passed through a bolter which consists of a silk-covered revolving cylinder made of wood several feet in length with an open end. The fine flour finds its way through the silk covering whilst the coarser bran and middlings pass out of the end of the cylinder and go as cattle feed.

A more modern alternative to a bolter is a dressing-machine which has sifters of very fine mesh wire through which the flour is screened into various grades.

Everything becomes very dusty in a mill and a coat of flour settles everywhere. For this reason an overdrift mill may be preferred. This means that the machinery is situated above the millstones. Consequently their well-greased cogs do not become as dusty as machinery that is situated underneath.

A miller must always keep his wits about him when his mill is operating taking particular care not to let the supply of corn stop. There is usually a warning bell fitted in the hopper above the stones. When sufficient grain is there a leather strap is kept down by the weight of grain. If it runs dry the strap rises and automatically starts the bell ringing.

CHAPTER 9

WEAVING AND LACEMAKING

HAND WEAVING

HAND WEAVING is a craft that has been practised all over the world for hundreds or even thousands of years. A wide variety of materials can be woven, those most commonly used being wool, cotton, flax, hemp and silk. In this country, wool was the usual material and in medieval times the craft was of national importance. To this day the Lord Chancellor sits on the woolsack in the House of Lords, commemorating the importance of this commodity. A very high degree of skill in hand weaving was attained helped by periodic influxes of Flemish weavers during times of persecution.

Weaving was a cottage industry until the coming of the industrial revolution when the processes were mechanised and the craft became concentrated in factories powered by coal-fired boilers. This resulted in development of the industry in the north of England and its depression in the southern counties where the only sort of power was that provided by water.

The hand weavers' existence became very precarious and their craft severely depleted until today their numbers have become insignificant in England though there are a few left in the remoter parts of Scotland and Wales.

There has however been a resurgence of the craft amongst the educated classes mostly as a hobby or as a means of making some money, though weaving is a slow business and it is almost impossible to make a living by it alone. Looms are still made and for around £100 a good large one can be purchased.

In England wool can be bought ready-spun but some people prefer to spin their own. The Wool Marketing Board have a monopoly and all fleeces have to be bought from a stapler who buys it from them.

Wool varies in quality, length of the staple, the part of the sheep from which it comes, the colour of the animal and its type of breed. The hand spinner has to pick over and sort the raw material to the weaver's requirements. At some stage it has to be washed, causing it to shed about a quarter of its weight in dirt and oil. Sometimes it

Carding wool

is scoured before spinning, although some people prefer to wash the wool after it has been spun.

First the wool has to be carded between a pair of carding boards fitted with innumerable small combs which lay the fibres parallel and turn the wool into a soft fleecy roving. These rovings may be attached to a distaff or fed by hand to the spinning wheel during the next operation. Hand-operated spinning wheels were supplanted by those worked by the foot during the nineteenth century. The spinning wheel converts the rovings into a twisted yarn, thin and long. A number of these yarns are in turn twisted together to form the thread used by the weaver. To keep up the supplies for the weaver's requirements, there were usually four spinsters. As spinning is a more time-consuming business than weaving a weaver nowadays buys most, if not all, of his wool ready-made as yarn.

Before use the wool is dyed. The dye may be derived from some vegetable source, being obtained from a very wide variety of plants such as lichens, bracken, woad, indigo and blackberry. Alternatively synthetic dyes are available in a wide range of colours.

The weaver makes a plan of the pattern he wishes to weave and then proceeds to set up his loom. The width of the weave depends on the requirement of the finished article whether it is to be a wide rug or mat, a suit width or a narrow one for a necktie. First the warp is set up, composed of yarns that run the length of the material which are wound around a warp beam. It may take a day or two to set up the loom, depending on the thickness of thread, width of material and the pattern required. Great care and concentration is required as any mistake makes the finished product quite unacceptable.

For the weft (the yarns that form the cross thread), yarns of the required colour are threaded on to shuttles and held in bobbins that revolve as the yarn is used.

When ready to start, the right tension is applied to the work by a ratchet device. By a movement of the foot the appropriate heddle is raised causing a previously selected number of yarns to be lifted thus forming a gap called a shed through which the shuttle is passed. By dropping the first heddle and raising another one a new shed is formed through which the shuttle is again passed in the reverse direction. By having a number of heddles and shuttles with different-coloured yarns a large number of permutations can be worked to form the desired pattern—an operation that requires both flair and concentration.

Each time the shuttle has passed through the shed the last weft yarn is beaten up tight. Occasionally a thread breaks causing a waste of time and skill to mend it and give the repaired thread the right tension. Continual care has to be taken to keep the edges, called selvages, of the cloth parallel. If the work has to be left for any time the tension of the warp has to be eased in order not to stretch the wool. Progress is inevitably rather slow particularly if the design is complicated so that in making a piece of patterned material 27 inches wide an average of a yard an hour might be made. Each length woven is about 15 yards long, the length that can conveniently be fitted on the warp roller.

Once the material is woven, it then has to be fulled to thicken and shrink the threads and give body to the finished cloth. This used to be done by treading in large vats or by hammering with wooden hammers in a water-operated fulling mill; fulling was always a separate craft and the first to be undertaken in a factory. The present-day home weaver can do it in the traditional manner by treading it in a bath. Finally it has to be steam pressed prior to a finishing process if needed. This may consist of raising the nap with teazles and shearing the surface smooth.

HAND-MADE LACE

Lace has been made in this country for several hundred years, influenced by Flemish, Dutch and Huguenot refugees. The work is very slow and requires a lot of concentration to avoid mistakes. Lacemaking, the exclusive preserve of women and young girls, offered very poor rewards and was little more than sweated labour. Most of the work was done at home frequently indoors by candlelight augmented by the condenser globes consisting of circular glass bowls filled with water that acted as lenses and concentrated the light. They are now sought after as antiques, rather like lacemakers' bobbins.

Lace can be made out of a number of materials including linen, cotton and silk, and in its day it was very fashionable for trimming the clothing of both men and women.

It is made on a pillow consisting of a large ball stuffed with hay and covered with any suitable material. Across the pillow the pattern is pinned tightly. The best patterns are made of pigskin parchment which last for years though they can be of other materials including paper. The pattern is pricked out in hundreds of holes about $\frac{1}{16}$ inch apart and into these are placed special lacemaking brass pins to outline the part of the pattern that is being worked.

The material of which the lace is made is wound on bobbins

Pillow lacemaking in progress

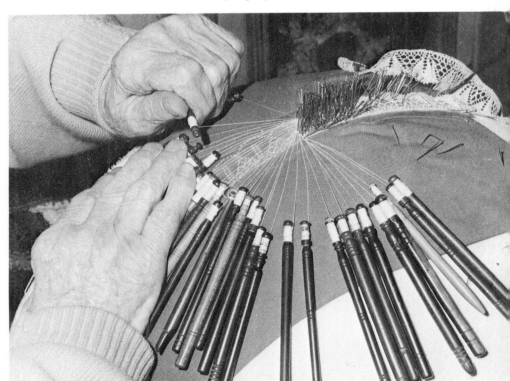

which are thin pencils of wood, or more rarely bone, round which the linen thread is tied with a slip knot to stop it unwinding. Any type of hardwood is used to make the bobbins which can be of beech, mahogany, oak or maple. Attractive ones inlaid with pewter were sometimes given by young men to their girl friends. There must be enough weight in the bobbins to give the required amount of tension to the thread and sometimes beads were tied to the ends to give a little extra weight. Some of the bobbins may have coloured tops to denote that they are runners which are the threads that run straight down the pattern as opposed to across it.

To make a stitch take two pairs of bobbins and carry out the following sequence of movements:

1　Take the two middle bobbins and put the left over the right,
2　Take the two outside bobbins and put right over left,
3　Cross the middle ones,
4　Twist the two outside ones over three times.

This operation makes one complete stitch.

The number of bobbins used depends on the width of the pattern being made and may vary from 30 to 100.

Mistakes show up badly so the work always has to be perfect with any error entailing a lot of unwinding to rectify. If a thread breaks or comes to an end a new one is joined by running it in and never by knotting.

Lacemakers become extremely adept and can work at great speed using both hands and carrying on a conversation at the same time.

Progress is slow and depends on the fineness of the thread being used. As a rough guide a square inch of lace might be produced in an hour.

When the end of the pattern has been reached there has to be a great upheaval as it is repositioned. The bobbins all have to be carefully gathered together and all the pins removed, probably around 100 of them. The pattern is then moved to its new position, the pins replaced, the bobbins put back in the right position and work is ready to start again, the whole operation taking about half an hour.

Making lace by hand as a living is probably dead in this country though it survives abroad. Some older members of the community still know how to do it and it is once more being practised as a hobby on an increasing scale.

CHAPTER 10

BASKET MAKING

BASKET MAKING is one of the oldest of crafts and is practised throughout the world using a wide variety of different materials such as willow, reed, rush, raffia, cane, etc.

In this country baskets are mostly from willows, frequently called osiers, which are specially grown for the purpose. Over the years progressively less has been produced and what is left is now largely confined to the flat low-lying areas of Somerset around Sedgemoor where the conditions are admirably suited to the purpose. The acreage has been falling alarmingly to about a tenth of the amount of fifty years ago and willow cultivators are depressingly gloomy about future prospects. The main difficulty is that a good deal of labour is required and with rising agricultural wages the cost is so high that an increasing amount of material is being imported as well as completed baskets to the detriment of the home industry. Unluckily the cultivation of basket willow does not readily lend itself to mechanisation.

Basket making with willows is an exclusively male occupation as

126

the work is hard on the hands and requires a good deal of strength in the arms particularly when using the thicker rods. Nearly all employees are paid by piece work on what they produce and they proceed at a good speed, but even so it is difficult to compete in price with imports though the quality of a good English basket is second to none and it will last a long time. There appear to be a number of young and middle-aged men in the craft, which although practised on a reduced scale now is far from dying.

Very adequate skill can be acquired in a year, whilst an income can be made from basket making almost at once. Not many tools are required and it suits men who may wish to be their own bosses. It is a craft, too, that can be practised by the blind or somebody with injured legs. The demand exceeds supply so the prospects look reasonable providing costs do not soar.

A skilled man can copy any pattern and the variety of shapes that can be produced is extensive. However most turn out the smaller articles to speed up output. This has resulted in such items as laundry baskets being in short supply.

WILLOW GROWING

Willows for baskets grow best in a well-drained land with a high watertable. To start a plantation the land has to be carefully prepared as for any other crop. Cuttings are put out in March. An 8-foot rod is cut into 14-inch lengths, 11 inches of which is pushed into the ground. The cuttings strike readily and are planted with a density of around 16,000 to the acre. Weeding is essential, and some is done mechanically in the early stages, but few growers can afford to do it as frequently as is desirable. The first- and second-year crop is worthless but the willows have to be cut to develop a good stool. From the third year onwards the crop is profitable. A plantation can last as long as forty years if well looked after, but this is rarely the case nowadays.

As the willow gets older more shoots are sent up which partially stifle the weeds, whilst the leaves that fall in the autumn mulch the ground. In early spring it is a common practice to graze cattle in the willow beds to keep down the weeds and they also eat the early shoots which might succumb to the frosts. Good clean rods are required without side shoots which are caused by the leading tips of the shoots becoming broken or damaged by wind or hail.

The harvesting is done in the winter by hand using a sickle to cut several rods at a time. They are then bundled, tied by a piece of willow using a rose knot that is quickly and skilfully formed by a combination of twisting the willow and turning it back on itself.

Of the great number of species and varieties of willow, only a very few are grown commercially. Most important is the *Salix trianda* variety, 'Black Maul' which has rods with little pith that are hard and pliable with a length of around 6 feet though this varies. It is the kind that predominates in Somerset. *Salix viminalis* grows to a height of up to 12 feet, suitable for use in coarser basketry whilst 'Champion' is left to grow for two years to produce a thicker rod for the 'sticks'.

PROCESSING THE WILLOW

Basket makers use three different types of rod, either brown, buff or white. Brown has the bark left on and the rougher stuff is used for this, whereas white and buff have the bark removed. White willow can be produced in one of two ways. Part of the crop can be left standing till the spring, and if cut during a short and critical period when the sap starts to rise, will peel without difficulty. Alternatively it can be cut and left standing in a ditch till the spring when it will peel comparatively easily. To obtain buff rods the willows are boiled for several hours with the bark still on and the tannin and other chemicals impart the characteristic and attractive red-brown colour.

The bark is removed in a brake which consists of a narrow V, formed by two pieces of metal. By pulling the bark through, it is stripped from the rod. The process can be greatly speeded by fitting a number of these brakes to a revolving drum and feeding in a bundle of around thirty rods. When one half has the bark removed they are withdrawn, reversed and the bark is removed from the rest of the rods.

Following the debarking, the rods are leant against wires or hedges out in the open to dry and turned periodically so that drying is even. When dry they are graded into lengths and types by placing in a tub and sorting into 4-, 5- and 6-foot lengths or whatever is required. Finally they are put into bundles measuring 3 feet around the butt, ready for dispatch to the purchaser.

WILLOW BASKETS

Basket makers perform their work sitting on a platform called a plank preferably made of elm and raised a few inches off the ground. The dimensions of the plank can vary but are generally about 3 feet long and 2 feet across. The worker usually has a shallow seat to give a little comfort. Sitting on his plank he places his legs apart either side of the lap board, a rectangular board which slopes away at a gentle incline. By his side are his ready-prepared willow rods which will have been soaked in water to make them pliable.

The tools of a basket maker

They may be left soaking for anything from a few hours up to a week depending on the type of willow and its thickness, the duration of soaking being judged by the experience of the basket maker. Before use they are removed from the water tank and left to mellow for some hours. The craftsmen only prepares sufficient rods for his daily use, an amount that has to be gauged by knowledge depending on the type of work in hand. A modest collection of tools are needed of which the following are the most important:

1　A knife to cut the end of the rods, to form slypes (grooves) and for trimming. Traditionally a shop knife is used but anything with a good cutting blade will serve.
2　A pair of secateurs to cut the larger sticks.
3　A beating iron to knock down the weave and keep it tight. This implement is a heavy piece of metal and may have an eye in one end which can be used for straightening rods.
4　A commander which is used for the same operation as a beating iron.
5　A bodkin used for making holes to insert rods. It may also be used for sticking through the bottom of a round or oval basket and through a hole in the lap board. The basket base revolves around it when slewing.
6　A screw block for clamping in sticks when making a square or rectangular lid or base of a basket.

Other requirements are a weight, frequently an old flat iron, to put in the bottom of a basket to keep it steady, some grease kept in a box or a horn to grease the bodkin, a yardstick for measuring, and possibly a cleaver and shave. The cleaver is for splitting a dry rod and it may have three or four vanes which give thin skeins. These are then pulled through the shave to trim them up and as a refinement the skeins might then be put through a special plane to get them to an exact width.

The first operation in making a basket is to prepare the bottom or base. A good foundation is essential as without it a basket will never be strong. For a round basket the slath is first formed. For example, three sticks, say 9 inches long, are placed on the lap board and a similar number are placed over these forming a cross. In order that they will lie flat on one another they are 'slyped'. This entails cutting a groove in them so they lie comparatively flat. Alternatively a hole is made through the centre of one trio and the other threaded through. A rod is then entwined around them moving in and out till they are bound together. The short sticks are bent so they point out radially like spokes from the centre of the base. More stakes are inserted between the weaving by sharpening the butt ends and pushing them in about 2 inches. The original two pairs of three sticks form twelve radials and if stakes are inserted each side of them there will be twenty-four. When a large enough base has been made, the weaving having been kept very tight which is an essential requirement at all stages, the stakes are pricked up. This entails bending them upwards with care being taken not to break them at the bend, a knack being needed for this manoeuvre. The base will have become saucer-shaped in the making so that it must be turned upside down before the pricking up. This will give the bottom of the basket a crown and it will stand firm and not wobble.

The next operation is 'upsetting'. Three rods are anchored into the base and worked round the vertical upset stakes in front of two then behind one, care being taken to keep the stakes equidistant. A hoop of willow will have been placed round the top of the stakes, its diameter depending on the final shape required. A variety of different-sized hoops is kept ready at hand.

After a few inches in height of upset work a variety of different weaves can be used. Randing is done with single rods being worked in and out. For this an even number of stakes are required. It is called slewing when between two and five rods are woven round an uneven number of stakes. In all operations new rods are let in as necessary and the ends cut in the final trimming.

All the time the work is banged down tight with the commander to keep it both even and symmetrical.

Various other strokes or weaves can be used—such as waling which is roughly similar to that used in upsetting, and fitching in

which a pair of rods is used to bind an openwork basket. The work in all basket making proceeds from left to right.

The different strokes produce a band of patterns which can be varied further by using white or buff rods or for rougher work, brown ones.

The basket is finished with a border formed by bending down the stakes and weaving them around the top, sometimes as a refinement with a flat finish. An oval basket presents a slightly more difficult problem in forming the slath of the base. To make this the craftsman usually stands up and anchors the sticks with his foot until enough weaving has taken place for it to hold together on its own.

Sometimes instead of using short sticks for the base some long rods are used and these eventually form the stakes and are pricked up. These are called ledgers and they give a basket added strength which is especially desirable if heavy weights are to be carried.

A somewhat different technique is required if the basket is rectangular or square and this is where the screw block is employed. A number of sticks are clamped in the block at regular intervals and rods are interwoven through these to form the base. It is then taken out of the clamp and trimmed. Sticks to form the sides are sharpened and pushed in as required at both ends whilst holes are made using the bodkin along the sides into which sticks are forced. After pricking up, the sides are then randed or slewed and the work continues the same as for an ordinary basket except that a good deal of care has to be taken to keep everything square.

The completed article is sometimes sprayed with varnish to give a shiny finish.

Frequently cane is also used, either alone or in combination with osier.

A good craftsman can make a very wide range of articles, copy anything with comparative ease, and achieve a series of identical products to fulfil a contract. Specialised baskets range from eel traps to lobster pots and swill and cran baskets for fishermen, but many that were formerly in general use in agriculture are no longer made owing to mechanisation and substitute materials. For example, potatoes are frequently mechanically harvested now, cutting out the need for baskets, but when they are picked by hand, cheaper wire containers are used. However there is still a place where the basket is supreme. This is in the fishing industry which needs a large number of swill baskets and, more important, quarter-cran baskets. The cran, about $3\frac{1}{2}$ hundredweight, is the official measure for herrings and the quarter-cran basket is the only recognised measurer of it. The size of this type of basket is rigidly laid down in accordance with the Cran Measure Act of 1908 and every single one is branded with the official stamp before being passed as fit for use for trade.

The 100-year-old Seabird Basket Works at Great Yarmouth has the virtual monopoly of making these, being the only firm big enough to turn them out in sufficient number. These baskets have a comparatively short life measured in weeks as they receive a lot of rough handling, are .nearly always wet, and expand with use, soon giving an over-weight of fish.

The Seabird works employs about nineteen men, many of them young, and is probably the biggest basket maker in the country turning out a wide range of goods but not coping with the demand. Nearly all other businesses dotted about all over England are much smaller.

SUSSEX TRUG BASKETS

The trug basket is peculiar to Sussex having been evolved by a resourceful man named Smith of Hurstmonceux who first showed them at the Great Exhibition of 1851. There they attracted the attention of Queen Victoria, and rapidly increased in popularity so that his descendants continue making them to this day. The somewhat curious name of trug is derived from the old English word for a boat whose shape they resemble. These strong, light and attractive baskets are made in a number of different sizes and are used all over the country by gardeners.

All are individually made by the twenty or so remaining crafts-men in the trade, retailing at a cost varying from about £1 for the smallest to several pounds for the biggest.

Their body is made of willow and the handle and rim of cleft chestnut or more rarely ash. Seasoning of the wood takes from six months to a year, and is to prevent shrinkage and warping in the basket. So many of the willow trees and chestnut coppices are being grubbed up so that the land can be put to more profitable use, that the wood is becoming much harder to obtain.

The trug makers are paid by piece work but the willow strips for the basket bodies are cut mechanically, this being the only part of the process that can be mechanised, and the chestnut for the frames is already cleft for them. The latter is done soon after cutting before sap rot sets in and then it is stored away to season. Each com-pleted basket has from five to seven flat willow slats or boards. After being cut by the mechanical saw they are then shaped by the craftsman sitting on a wooden horse and using a draw knife. All this is done by eye with the craftsman's experience shaping the pieces to the exact requirements needed. The ends of the long thin slats are slightly reduced in thickness and curved so that they almost make a point. Before assembly can take place all the pieces are put into a steam oven to make them pliable for bending to shape. After about five minutes in the oven they are removed and ready for bending between the blocks which consist simply of two bars of wood with a gap between. A bundle of slats is placed between the bars and bent, an operation that takes about a minute, so pliable does the wood become. The boiler fire is kept alight by the unwanted shavings so that nothing goes to waste.

The handles and rims are bent round a wooden former and cut to the required dimensions for the particular size of basket that is being made. First the handles are made and clenched with a galvanised clout nail, the rim being similarly formed and the two nailed together. All is then ready for the willow bodywork. The slats which have been bent are put in place and fixed in position using copper nails, having been previously dipped in water to keep them pliable and non-slippery. First the bottom slat is nailed in position. The next slat is fitted slightly overlapping the first being placed inside it and so on till the top of the rim is reached. When all the slats have been secured in position the protruding ends are trimmed flush with the rim.

Finally a pair of pieces of willow are nailed on underneath to form a stand and the trug is then complete, each one being an individual work of art in itself. Depending on the size about twelve to eighteen can be made in a day by each man—not enough to satisfy the demand.

SPALE BASKETS

Spale baskets, sometimes called spelks, swills, skips, or wiskets, have been produced in the Furness area of Lancashire for over 200 years, but their production has now tailed off drastically. They are

made out of interwoven rent oak strips and have served a very wide variety of purposes as they are strong, rigid, comparatively light and durable, and used to be very cheap. Mostly they were used for potato gathering, coaling skips and a wide variety of other purposes on the farm including cattle feeding for which one end was made shallower than the other.

Today a mere handful of men, all of them old, are left making them and it appears that in another decade there will be no swillers left. Though the craft is dying there are no special secrets about their construction and some enterprising person could rejuvenate it and be sure of a demand far in excess of supply.

There is only one firm of three men all nearing their pensions

(Opposite) A spale basket maker using a mare to trim his wood. This is usually done mechanically nowadays

who make their living from the craft and this is run by Mr Fred
Baines, the last indentured man in the business who completed
his five-year apprenticeship some years before the war. No young
people want to enter the trade. This organisation turns out around
forty-eight baskets a week with orders on hand for six months and
work having to be turned away. In 1930 they were made for 18p
and in 1972 their price has risen to just over £2.

The rims of the baskets are made of a single length of hazel
which has been boiled to make it pliable and then bent round a
wooden former of the required size and secured with a nail. Three
sizes are now made—20, 22 or 24 inches—the measurement being
the length of the baskets. For the bodywork, oak in its green state
is bought and cut into lengths about 4 feet long with a diameter
of about 1 foot. It is then cleft into narrow wedges with a lath axe,
more often called a froe in other districts, and when required for
use is boiled for six hours (the exact time is not critical) to make it
pliable. An opening is made using a bill hook, the back of which is
hit with a wooden mallet and an oak lath is then pulled off by hand
with a width of 2 or 3 inches, a length of 4 feet and a thickness of a
little less than $\frac{1}{4}$ inch. It is then put in a machine that cuts the thickness in half making laths a little over $\frac{1}{16}$ inch thick which are then
planed smooth in another machine. Previously this had to be done
by hand with the operator using a mare to hold the lath which he
smoothed with a draw-knife.

Enough wood is prepared to last the week, the preparation now
taking two days whereas before it took half the week.

In making the basket the craftsman sits on his stool, takes the
hazel rim and with his knife makes a slit to take a lath. The laths
are all placed by his side and have to be moist to make them pliable.
The ribs or spills are all fixed in position first and then the taws
which go lengthways are woven in starting with thin laths on the
sides of the baskets and thick ones for the bottom. The weaving
of these taws starts in the centre of the basket and when the rim is
reached they are wound round it in a complete turn and then laced
back, the end skilfully hidden under a rib. When the baskets dry

out the laths set hard, making the whole construction very rigid and strong.

The basket is shaped by eye and the finished product will have the laths close enough together to enable it to hold grain without any dropping out.

The employees are paid on the number of baskets they turn out and they can make a basket in an hour. They prepare all their own material which needs care, as broken or split laths cause delays and therefore a loss of money. Some of the laths in the closing stages have to be trimmed to shape to get a good fit and to avoid holes in the bottom of the basket.

RUSH BASKETS

There is a small amount of rushwork still made commercially in England, chiefly in East Anglia. The material is comparatively cheap, little equipment is needed and as it is quite soft and pliable, it is easily worked by women without being hard on the hands.

The rush that is used exclusively, the bulrush *Scirpus lacrustus*, can be found growing throughout the country by rivers and streams. The rushes are collected by tradition between the hay and corn harvest but not before the longest day; if left they die off in the autumn. After harvesting they are dried very carefully, an operation that must be done correctly because if too dry they become brittle and if left moist turn mouldy.

They are sold by the bolt, with a length of 7 feet and about 30 inches round, which makes them rather bulky to transport. The supplies that are produced commercially in England do not satisfy the increasing demand and some are imported from Holland which are somewhat harder and not so pleasant to work.

To make articles like bags or hats it is easiest to make them over a wooden former of the required shape. First the rushes are interlaced, over one and under one, being held initially by drawing pins. The interweaving continues following the contours of the former and is finished off by a row of waling or plaiting.

With practice, a degree of.dexterity can be acquired comparatively easily and more ambitious designs executed. The work can be done on the flat to make articles like table-mats.

Another method is to plait the reed into long lengths. These are then wound round a former and held in shape by string which is threaded through the plait using a sacking needle. Log baskets and flour mats can be made by this method.

More and more amateurs are making articles out of rushes so that now they are not always easy to obtain.

POTTERY

POTTERY is one of the most ancient of rural village crafts, practised since time immemorial. Due to its weight, clay is not easily transported and potteries must be sited near a supply of raw material. Clay varies in texture and chemical content so that a suitable kind can be found only by trial and error.

The finished products of the potter are frequently large and transport problems before the arrival of turnpikes and canals encouraged the growth of a large number of rural local potteries making such items as jugs, urns, all sorts of containers, flower pots, chimney pots, etc.

With modern factory-made substitutes the number of traditional potteries has become sadly depleted. They have been replaced largely by artist potters who cater for the requirements of those who prefer individually created hand-made articles. There is a steady demand for these, particularly as the prices are, on the whole, reasonable.

A potter, having obtained his clay, has to do a good deal of preparation to get it ready for use. First it has to be pugged to mix it

up and remove pebbles and shells. The next operation is to wedge it by kneading with the hands to get rid of air bubbles and obtain an even consistency.

Articles can be made either by moulding by hand or alternatively on a circular revolving wheel, the latter having been introduced to this country by the Celts.

When using a wheel the first operation is to throw a lump of prepared clay on to the centre of the revolving disc. The amount has to be very exact for the article that is to be thrown. It has either to be weighed or judged by experience. A wheel may be operated by foot or be electrically driven, depending on the preference of the potter, but if large pieces are being made, nearly a ton of clay can be handled in the course of a day. In this case it is less tiring physically to have an electric wheel. Once the lump of clay is centred on the wheel, it is next raised using the fingers and thumb and skilfully manipulated into the required shape, with the base and sides being kept of an even thickness. Whilst altering the required curvature of the outside of the vessel the potter's hands have to be kept moist and a sponge is generally used to help with the finishing touches. On completion a thin piece of wire is run under the article to detach it from the wheel so that it can be laid aside to dry. This is an important stage during which the clay shrinks by about an eighth and has to take place away from draughts and extremes of temperature in order not to split it.

Quite large pots can be raised on a wheel, the maximum size depending on the length of the potter's arm. The size can be increased by joining two pieces together and replacing on the wheel when they have dried out a little. It is possible to use as much as 70 pounds of clay for the largest pieces.

In the past chimney pots were made in large numbers, but these are now mostly produced by machinery which extrudes the pot giving it parallel sides and a less attractive appearance on a roof top.

(Opposite) A potter shaping a giant-sized pot on his wheel

When the clay has dried leather hard, handles and other decoration can be applied by the use of some slip consisting of a suspension of liquid clay.

MOULDING

Articles that are not created on a wheel can be formed into the required shape in moulds. These can be made of plaster of Paris or carved out of wood. The clay is pressed into these and when it shrinks in drying becomes detached from the mould whence it is easily removed. Sizeable moulded segments can be joined together to form a single unit and small moulded pieces of decoration can be added to a pot by fixing it with slip.

FIRING

The firing is done in a kiln to the required temperature. A low temperature gives a soft porous pot whilst a higher one vitrifies the clay to stone.

Originally the fires were all wood with the temperatures comparatively low resulting in the finished article being slightly porous which is perfectly satisfactory for such items as chimney and flower pots. If they have to be watertight, a glaze is applied which usually requires a second firing at a greater temperature.

Coal eventually replaced wood as a firing material, followed by oil and sometimes electricity which enables higher temperatures to be reached coupled with much better control.

All kilns have a spyhole for observation and the heat can be regulated according to requirements and judged either by experience or by using indicators that melt at a known temperature.

The rural craftsmen's kilns were usually shaped in the form of a large bottle made of brick, with wedge-shaped saggars taking the weight of the contents. In packing the kiln the clay articles must have lost most of their water content by being left to dry for around two weeks though the time varies with the conditions under which this process takes place.

The kiln has to be very carefully loaded and stacking needs to be skilfully done so that for economic reasons the maximum load can be fired.

When fully loaded the entrance to the kiln is sealed up with clay and the furnace is lit. For a day or two the heat has to be very gentle in order that the remaining moisture can slowly dry out. After that the full heat is applied for a similar period then reduced so the contents can cool down slowly. Too rapid a change of temperature at the start or finish of the operation can cause considerable damage and cracking with a consequently high percentage of loss to say nothing of the waste of time and material. Impurities in the clay such as small stones or shells that have escaped detection in the preparation stage can create havoc by exploding in the kiln and damaging the surrounding articles.

LEATHER

TANNING IS the process in which a skin is turned into leather to preserve it. Tanning has been practised for thousands of years and can be done in a variety of different ways including soaking in solutions or by rubbing oil into the skin. The solution can be inorganic or vegetable. Most plants and trees contain tannin and in this country the most commonly used vegetable solution was that made from oak bark.

Some 200 years ago there were small tanneries in very large numbers all over the country dealing with the valuable skins of any slaughtered cattle. The leather was used for saddlery, boots, clothing, drinking vessels, covering books and a whole host of other items. Gradually the tanneries have been closing over the years and the remaining ones have become bigger, more mechanised and tan with different solutions.

One of the most common involves chrome which has so speeded up the process that it takes a few days to tan the leather instead of the months or even a year needed for oak bark tanning. Chrome tanning has been used for nearly 100 years and the repercussions are obvious, taking into account the vast amounts of leather now needed for footwear alone and the volume that has to be produced. Millions of pounds have been spent in the search for alternatives for leather, but although some substitutes have been found nothing as yet has proved to be better than leather for footwear and saddlery. The prestige of leather is such that items made from it are frequently advertised as 'solid leather'. Even after tanning leather remains porous which is why it is used so extensively for shoes, gloves and clothing.

Much of the vegetable tanning materials are imported from abroad and arrive in concentrated form which helps with transport. Probably the most widely used is quebracho from a South American tree. Another comes from wattle bark from Natal.

OAK BARK TANNING

Only one or two tanneries have survived in England which use the rather slow oak bark process and there is a good deal of difficulty in obtaining the raw material in spite of the number of oaks that are felled annually. The best tannin comes from the bark of young trees which were readily available in the past when there were plenty of oak coppices. Now they have almost entirely disappeared. These were cut about every twenty-five years. Tannin comes chiefly from the inner part of the bark and for this reason there was a great deal of wastage if the bark came from old trees and had become thick and gnarled. Bark is most easily peeled when the sap is rising in spring and early summer. This, unfortunately, is the least favoured time for cutting wood as it takes longer to season, though this objection is nowadays of far less importance due to modern kiln drying. The bark is levered off the tree using a barking iron consisting of a tool with a handle and chisel-pointed blade, a slit is made, the tool inserted and a cylinder of bark is levered off coming away quite easily. As soon as possible the bark is stored under cover, so that the tannin is not washed out by the rain.

With the very small present-day demand for bark and the high labour costs few merchants bother to remove it so the tanneries have to find it where they can, irrespective of the age of the trees it came from. As an indication of the amount required, one of the biggest users, Bakers of Colyton in Devon needs 25 tons a year.

To prepare the tannin solution the bark is put through a machine that shreds or minces it up. A quantity is then put in a large tank, fresh water is added and the secretions in the bark are dissolved leaving a dark-brown tanning solution. The density of this is measured by a hydrometer and when it has reached the required strength it is drawn off ready for use. As a generalisation it is only worth while tanning top-quality hides almost entirely free from blemishes. Hides may be damaged by warble fly, which puncture it, horn wounds, barbed wire scratches or flay marks caused by careless skinning. The quality of a hide depends on a variety of factors such as the age of the animal and the quality of the pasture.

The hides arrive at the tannery with hair on one side and a certain amount of fat and flesh adhering to the other.

The hairs are first removed by soaking the hide in a solution of lime which loosens them and they can then be scraped off with a long knife with a handle at each end. The surplus fat and flesh is then trimmed off the underside. Nothing is wasted, the hair being used for felt and the trimmings for gelatine. For this operation the hide is put over a large block of wood with a circular diameter placed so as to slope away from the operator who does his work by pushing his scudding knife away from him. Thence the hides are thrown into a tank to neutralise the preservative before being taken to the tanning pits which are some 5 feet in depth and 8 feet square and made of board lined with clay. Every hide is suspended at each end, attached to a wooden rod and lowered into the pit containing the tanning solution until totally submerged. Each pit takes about fifty. There are from a dozen to twenty of these pits with varying densities of tannin which are regularly tested for strength. The hides are put into the weaker solution to begin with to ensure even tanning. If a strong solution was used at the start the outside would become tanned and not the inside. The hides are passed through a succession of pits for about three months ending up by being laid flat in the solution and piled up one on top of the other for the final part of the tanning. The whole process takes about nine months with a slight variation depending on the strength of the solutions and the temperature, less time being taken in warm weather. All this is judged by experience and requires a high degree of skill that takes years to acquire. The hides are then bleached to bring them to a light-brown colour. A difficulty is caused by the fact that not only are all hides slightly different but they vary in thickness with the skin from the animal's back being the thickest part. Sometimes large pieces of leather are required for upholstery or saddlery whilst for bootmaking the dimensions can be smaller and hides are cut or trimmed as required. This in itself demands expertise in order that the hides are cut in the most economical way.

The hide has to be very carefully dried under controlled conditions to prevent it cracking if dried too quickly or going mouldy if too slowly.

It is subjected to a number of other processes such as scrubbing, rubbing in oil, rolling to compress the fibres and smooth out the wrinkles and then put through a shaving machine to give it an even thickness overall, the excess material being removed from the flesh side of the hide.

Next comes the currying or dressing of the leather which takes approximately another three months. This is a craft of its own and is sometimes undertaken by a specialist firm. For saddlery and harness the leather is scrubbed either mechanically or by hand and set out when still wet using an instrument called a slicker which is shaped like a scraper with a blunt edge and makes the hide lie quite flat with particular attention being paid to the edges.

The hide is then hung up to dry and later reset. When dry it is whitened on the flesh side of the leather and boshed (ie coated and rubbed) with a mixture of boiled tapioca, then glassed off with the cutting edge of a piece of glass.

Afterwards it is stained to the required shade either black or some tone of brown by brushing on the colour. Finally mutton tallow is applied to both sides and left to soak for a few weeks. When the leather is required for use, the tallow is removed and the butts are despatched to the saddler invariably being sold by the pair. By this time the leather will have spent a year in the tannery undergoing the various treatments. Leather from the belly is slightly thinner than the back but nevertheless of good quality and none is wasted.

Though harness leather is ready when it leaves the factory it matures and continues to improve and a knowledgeable saddler keeps a small stock and uses it when just right.

The making of shoe leather is slightly different though this is mostly technical such as cutting the hide differently and using another rolling technique as well as a number of secret processes or tricks of the trade. Though the hides are top quality they may have slight blemishes; but these pieces can be used as insoles or heels to avoid waste. Shoe leather is sold in 'bends' by the weight.

There is not a great deal of oak-bark tanned shoe leather still produced but all the production there is goes into top-quality footwear as it is more expensive and probably wears better than other leather though modern methods of tanning have been steadily improving and the difference is not very great.

Oak bark tanning is one of the most specialised of the ancient crafts. The methods and techniques evolved over several hundred years have led to the very high degree of proficiency.

SADDLERY

Saddlery is a very ancient craft and has remained much the same since medieval times with only minor changes in design and technique.

Over the years the craft became divided into three separate but allied sections: saddle making, collar making and harness making, given in order of prestige. In a small concern the three can all be done by one man.

The equipment turned out today is mostly for the comparatively wealthy who are prepared to pay a fair price. The most expensive to buy initially is probably the cheapest in the long run and certainly if looked after will last very many years. It also keeps its appearance and still looks attractive after years of wear. It is possible to do saddlery with comparatively few tools, but in practice most saddlers have a large number each of which is used for a particular job to speed up the work, although nothing can be hurried. These tools do not wear out very rapidly and in most cases the older saddlers will have had most of them all their careers and are quite likely to have inherited them. They are always kept close at hand and losses are few.

All the tools and equipment such as saddle trees and buckles are made in Walsall where a number of saddles are also produced. What is left of the trade is in a fortunate position today. It is difficult to keep up with the home requirements let alone the possibility of exporting anything in spite of a world-wide demand for British saddles.

The leather used is always of the top quality and sold direct from the tanners to the saddlers, mutual confidence having been built up over the years.

The best and strongest fittings are made of stainless steel for preference. Nickel is less expensive, but nevertheless very serviceable.

All leather equipment needs maintenance with a regular application of saddle soap to keep it supple and in good condition.

In the past the bulk of a saddler's work was connected with harness for horses used in agriculture. An assured market, including a great deal of repair work, existed for some hundreds of years until the present century. From the 1920s onwards trade became very depressed with prospects most discouraging for apprentices. The harness-making side of saddlery has never recovered and has almost ceased to exist but saddle makers are beginning to prosper again with the horse population once more increasing. Evidence of this is to be seen in the larger fields at hunts, a vast increase in the numbers of children's ponies and a steady rise in the popularity of racehorses with about 11,000 now in training. Television coverage of show jumping and cross-country events not to mention royal patronage has helped to encourage riding.

SADDLE MAKING

The production of saddles is divided between small firms dotted about the country and larger workshops where some form of line production is worked. There is virtually no scope for mechanisation so that the finished article depends almost entirely on the skill of the saddler. A good saddle can take one man nearly a week to make but as a rule not all operations are done by a single individual except in a very small business.

The actual method of making a saddle has changed very little through the centuries. This is partly due to the craftsmen being very conservative and partly because no better methods or new materials have presented themselves. Plastic and nylon have so far not been developed to play any significant part in their making which is

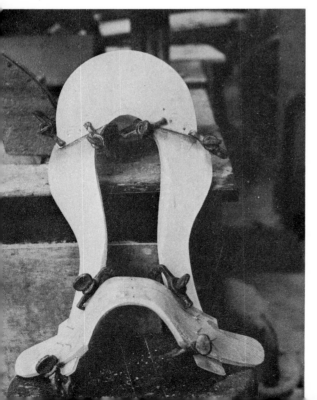

Pieces of a laminated saddle tree clamped together

mostly of very good quality leather. The best saddle seats are of pigskin which is largely produced in Scotland and are fitted with the grainy side uppermost whilst the rest of the saddle is of cowhide though serge or linen can be substituted on the underside of the seat to reduce cost.

Originally all the leather was oak bark tanned but over the years this method has become rarer and an increasing amount of chemical-tanned leather is being used. During the last twenty years great strides have been made in this type of tanning and the leather produced is of superb quality.

The foundation of a saddle is the tree which is a skeleton of laminated beech wood with some metal parts and two drop forged spring stirrup bars attached one in each side to take the leathers and allow them to be released in the event of the rider being thrown with his foot still in the stirrup.

A tree may look quite a simple piece of construction but a close examination shows it to be a very intricate article requiring a high degree of specialised skill to manufacture. A few are now being made of plastic and fibreglass but the majority are of laminated beech or occasionally birch. The framework is hot moulded in two, three or four pieces depending on the style required, and glued together, later to be put in a vice for final shaping with draw knives and files, an operation that takes about a quarter of an hour. A variety of types are required for hunting, show jumping and racing, and different sizes have to be made in each category.

A modern variant that is being made in significant numbers is the spring steel tree. The spring is given by a piece of steel and the wooden framework is reduced in width to allow some give. After shaping the tree has a covering of canvas glued over it and finally the metal fittings are riveted on. The majority are made in Walsall with demand severely taxing the supply.

This is the sequence for making a saddle:

1   Web and serge the tree by tacking webbing over it and covering with serge.

2   Cut out from the quality leather the seat, skirt, flaps and panels. The latter can be made of linen and serge for initial cheapness but have to be renewed quite often.

3   Welt the seat to the skirt.

4   Sew on girth straps.

5   Fix flaps.

6   Attach seat to the tree.

7   Make panel and stuff it partially.

8   Fix panel to saddle.

9   Complete stuffing and quilt it.

Whilst all the operations in saddle making require a degree of skill, the ultimate quality of the work shows up in the stretching which has to be neat, regular and hand done with between nine and twelve stitches to the inch. The stitch holes are first made by a pricking iron or punch which is fitted with a row of about a dozen

Stuffing the padding of a saddle below the seat

pins. A hammer blow on the top causes the pins to puncture the leather and leave a row of holes correctly spaced ready to be enlarged with an awl. Alternatively if the stitching is on a curve then a pricking wheel is used to mark the stitch holes.

The thread is invariably spun from strands made up by each individual saddler and is of the best flax liberally coated with beeswax. In hand stitching two needles are used, one taking the thread down the hole in the leather and the other bringing a second thread up. Should a thread break or wear through it will not run back as in machine stitching. A well-cared-for, top-quality saddle will last a very long time, anything from fifty to a hundred years during which time some of the stitching may have to be renewed and the padding will need to be repacked periodically.

The best saddles weigh about 8 pounds and may cost anything up to £140. Considering the time it will last, it is a comparatively cheap price to pay and not a great deal in relation to the expense of purchasing a horse and feeding it. Moreover it retains its price well and will fit any horse of a similar type providing it has no abnormal features.

Any good quality hand-stitched saddle at its cheapest is bound to cost around £70, made up as follows, the figures being very approximate: cost of tree £5; materials £15; labour £30; profit and overheads £20. It will be noted that the labour cost is the biggest element.

Reins and stirrup leathers must always be of the highest quality as any breakage might cause an unpleasant accident. In this part of the equipment the stitching is vitally important and may need renewing after some years. In particular wear will take place where the leather holds the stirrup, especially if the length never has to be adjusted and all the wear occurs in the same place.

Saddle makers remark somewhat ruefully that their saddles last too long. However, as the market is expanding appreciably at the present time this does not matter. In any case only just over half the time is spent on new work and the rest on repairs. Good saddlers mostly have work on their hands for six months ahead and if the output was stepped up all the surplus could be exported with ease as there is a great demand for English saddlery abroad which cannot be met. English saddles are produced at half the cost of those made in France.

The making of racing saddles is a specialised form of saddlery. The rules state that there must be a saddle, but one of under one pound weight can suffice. Racehorses have a special lightweight saddle for exercising which weighs about $5\frac{1}{2}$ pounds. The very few firms who make this type of equipment are all situated near racing stables or training grounds.

Saddlery, although once again an expanding business, is not a craft that can raise its output appreciably as it takes a number of years for a craftsman to acquire the full range of skills. An apprenticeship takes four years but an apprentice can begin to earn his keep after about a month. Luckily it is a profession with some attractions and a small but steady trickle of youth is entering the craft. Working conditions are good and the wages adequate bearing in mind that any skilled men are generally paid a good deal more than the rather meagre laid-down rate. The work is variable, interesting and non-repetitive so is never dull, and if doing repair work an apprentice can see for himself the standard of craftsmanship of the original maker. Like all the best craftsmen, saddlers are proud of their work and have the satisfaction of being able to see their results as they go along.

There is invariably a shop attached to a saddlery which frequently means there has to be an attendant so that the craftsmen are not repeatedly disturbed. It is probably uneconomical for a saddler to sell only his own production so the usual practice is to buy in other goods, usually of leather, in order to increase the volume of items for sale.

The statistics of saddlers over the last half century are interesting. In 1920 there were 12,000 saddlers whilst by 1957 the number had dwindled to 600 and during the same time the horse population had dropped from $1\frac{1}{2}$ million to 60,000. During this period the horse has virtually ceased to be used for haulage and agriculture but in compensation the numbers of racehorses, ponies and hunters has been increasing appreciably particularly in the last decade.

COLLAR AND HARNESS MAKING

This section of the saddlery craft has suffered a dramatic decline during the present century from a very strong and thriving trade to being virtually non-existent except for three or four businesses who are really interested and prepared to undertake this work at the present time. It is ironical that the pressure of work on the survivors is considerable with orders in hand for six months ahead and business having to be turned away. There are a number of older saddlers who can make and repair harness but may decline to do so as the equipment is a little different and collar making is a specialised craft in itself.

The main requirement is for hackney and show harness where a high-class turnout is essential. There is also a small demand for working horses such as brewers' drays and for heavy farm horses which are slowly beginning to increase in numbers after reaching a low point a few years ago.

A selection of horse collars in various stages of completion

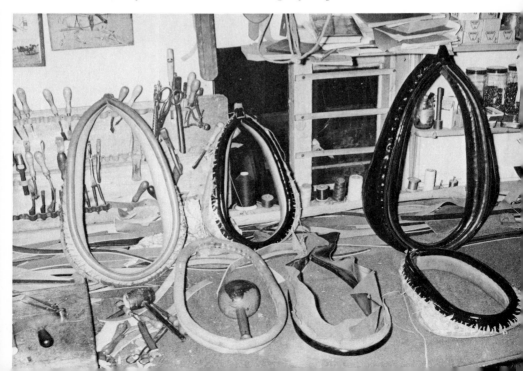

It is only worth making top-quality equipment as the labour is almost the same as for a less good article. Most of the stitching is at ten to the inch though in the past the finest used to be fourteen to sixteen to the inch when labour and harness makers were plentiful. A few items such as blinkers, noseband and traces, can be machine stitched, but all the rest is done by hand.

To make a good collar requires a masterly touch. They are made in a number of sizes to fit the various breeds of horse and consist of a variety of pieces to make up the completed unit. First there is the wale consisting of a tube or roll of leather tightly packed with rye straw. Although it is not particularly easy to obtain today, rye straw is invariably used, because it is 5 or 6 feet long, very resilient and does not rot. The wale is put around a collar block, a tall tapering piece of wood with a cross section similar to a horse's neck, small at the top for light horses and thick lower down for heavier breeds. Every horse should have its own collar which conforms to the shape of each animal. For preference there should be two collars for each horse so that one can be allowed to dry out or be repaired. Collars are best made after harvest when a horse's muscles and condition are at their peak. The block gives the wale its correct shape. To the wale is stitched the body of the collar which is tightly packed with straw and some flock and sewn up tight. It may be all of leather or alternatively lined on the inside with serge. For most of this work the leather is moistened in order to get a good fit and to shrink tight around the straw stuffing. Finally come the hames which fit between the wale and the body and to which are attached the harness fittings. These are factory made, normally of mild steel and frequently brass plated. In the past they were sometimes made of ash with metal fittings. They usually have a small chain at the bottom and are strapped together at the top. They have a pair of rings to thread the reins through and a pair of hinged tug hooks that take the tug or the trace chain. As the whole of the pushing power of the horse is thrown against the collar it is essential that it should be a good and comfortable fit. The leather for heavy work is usually dyed black and treated with cod oil to keep it supple. Collars are normally measured by the inside length and can be as long as 25 inches for a large shire horse, with a weight of 20 pounds. They always have to be put on upside down in order to pass over the top of the head, being the widest part, and then turned the correct way up. It takes about fifteen hours to make a good show collar which will then last anything from twenty-five to fifty years, depending on the amount it is used and the care taken.

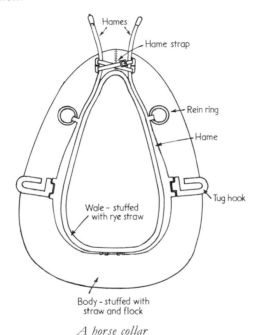

Hames

Hame strap

Rein ring

Hame

Tug hook

Wale – stuffed with rye straw

Body – stuffed with straw and flock

A horse collar

Show harness consists largely of patent leather most of which has to be imported from Germany. It is made by a special process, being lacquered with about seven coats which are sprayed on the reverse side of the leather giving it the characteristic very high gloss finish. Most of the remainder of the leather is oak bark tanned.

Recently costs have been soaring faster than ever before. The price of leather has about doubled inside a year and all other items have increased correspondingly. The final cost used to consist of about a quarter for material, a quarter labour, a quarter overheads and a quarter profit. The cost of a collar goes by the size at £1.50 an inch so a big one would be £40 whilst a complete set of harness would cost a minimum of £150. This is not a very great price bearing in mind the quality of the work, the life of the harness and the relative value of the horse together with its equipment.

Nowadays, most of it is for show and the hobby enthusiast.

HORSE BRASSES

The final embellishing touches to the harness is the brass ornamentation. Brass decoration is frequently let in to the blinkers, nose and brow band and may be inscribed with the owner's name or initials.

Brasses became a feature of cart horses and a heavy animal sometimes carries about 6 pounds of them. They are carried on the forehead, martingale and anywhere else where there is a vacant space on the leather. The old carters were very proud of them. They were owned by the carter though probably paid for by the owner or farmer of the horse and represented lucky charm signs and ancient

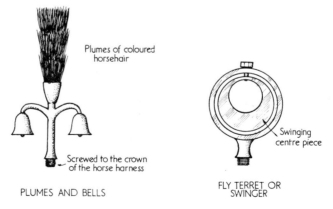

Plumes of coloured horsehair

Screwed to the crown of the horse harness

PLUMES AND BELLS

Swinging centre piece

FLY TERRET OR SWINGER

Harness ornaments

symbols to ward off the evil eye, although in later days were worn purely as ornaments.

Brasses began to get popular during the Napoleonic Wars and became quite a feature during the later Victorian days. The early ones were stamped or cut out of sheet metal and later they were cast. They are still being made today for interior decoration though they are usually rougher than the ones that have been used on harness not having been worn smooth by use nor having acquired a patina.

Other decoration included a fly tarret or swinger surmounted with a plume worn on the crown of the horse and another on the saddle sometimes with swinging ornaments or with tinkler bells. Alternatively a set of bells or rumblers was carried above the collar and these gave a warning to approaching traffic which was helpful in a winding lane.

BOOTMAKING

The village cobbler, once a prominent and necessary member of the community has all but disappeared so that the remaining craftsmen are almost all in the towns. Here most of the work is taken up in doing repairs rather than making shoes as the latter has been so successfully mechanised.

Before the advent of mass-produced, ready-made shoes earlier in the century every village with a population of about 300 people was able to support a shoemaker. A pair of boots or shoes take approximately a day to make so that if every villager had a new pair a year it would give full employment to one man.

The making of hand-made shoes is a very skilled and specialised craft. The various operations are frequently done by different operators though the feasibility of doing this depends on the size of the business and the number of men available.

In making a shoe, first the feet have to be measured, there being a slight variation in size and shape in almost every individual. A pair of lasts then has to be made the exact shape of the feet. Beech wood is invariably used for this as it does not warp. The lasts are either bought or cut slightly undersize so that they can be built up to the correct dimensions by gluing on pieces of leather which are finally smoothed off by using sandpaper.

The clicker is then able to start his work cutting out the leather for the uppers on his special hardwood cutting board built up of sections of wood which have the grain running vertically. He cuts the leather to the best advantage to avoid wastage, particularly as leather prices have more than trebled in the last two years. For shoe uppers calf or kid leather is generally used to give softness and suppleness. This is bought by the square foot and may be black in which case it is called box calf (taking its name from the berries of the box tree which used to provide the dye) or brown willow calf, which is dyed by willow. The shoe linings can be made out of the less good pieces of leather though canvas or linen can be substituted. The uppers are sewn together either by silk or nylon thread and then passed on for the operation of lasting.

The uppers are placed on the last which is fixed over a bench in an upside-down position, the inner sole laid across the top. The uppers are held to this by the temporary use of tacks. A bracing of thread is next passed through the leather all around the circumference to hold it in position over the last ready for the next operation, either the sewing on of the welt or sticking on of a sole. The exact techniques vary in detail with each individual but the final result looks the same. Whereas the thread used on the uppers is bought ready made on reels, the craftsmen make up their own threads for stitching the soles from thin strands of hemp with seven to ten cores depending on the thickness needed. The strands are rolled together on the thigh with a pig bristle from the hair of a wild boar, or a nylon substitute cunningly affixed to both the finished ends to enable it to be pulled through the holes made by the awl. The thread is waxed for preservation and easier working.

The leather used for the soles is far heavier and less flexible than that for the uppers. It is bought either by the butt or by bends, each butt consisting of two bends. This leather is bought by weight at a cost of £1 a pound and it may have been tanned by the oak bark method, now getting rare, or one of the newer and quicker processes. The butt is the tanned skin of an animal and varies in quality and size with each individual, just as the skin varies depending on the part of the anatomy that it covered. Thus the belly is less good than the back. The latter is therefore used for the soles and the former for insoles and heels with virtually no wastage of material. A butt produces about fifty pairs of soles which have to be evenly matched for thickness and quality.

For cheaper and lighter shoes the soles are glued on. The uppers are cross stitched over the insole and the gap filled in with a composition material or tarred felt that is trimmed level. Before this a metal shank several inches long is tacked to the insole to keep up and strengthen the instep of the finished shoe. A certain amount of trimming takes place at all stages and a razor-sharp knife is of paramount importance. It is stropped at frequent intervals and is worn out after a few weeks as it is in continual use.

The soles are glued on under pressure and heat. For making a welted shoe the final procedure is altogether different. The insole has a feather cut all around it about $\frac{1}{4}$ inch in depth and this is turned up to form a thin wall of leather all the way round. Taking his awl, possibly having first dipped it in beeswax, the craftsman pushes it under this wall, through the shoe upper and a thin strip of leather called the welt which encompasses the shoe and to which the sole is finally sewn. Through the awl hole is passed the bristle taking the thread. Another awl hole is made and the thread passed back whilst the other end is threaded in the opposite direction to form a lock stitch of which there are between four and six to the inch. When the welt has been sewn on all round the bottom of the shoe is carefully trimmed and the middle filled in the same manner as for a stuck-on sole.

The sole is then dampened and a channel cut all round it for taking the thread. It is then glued to hold it in position and hammered to the shoe with a driver, a steel tool like a heavy-duty file, ready for the final stitching. This is occasionally done by hand with

about six stitches to the inch but more frequently by machine. The raised piece of leather formed in cutting the channel is pressed back over the stitching to hide and protect it. The heels are hammered on and the shoes are then given the final touches.

Hand-made shoes are not cheap. It pays to use the very best leather which is expensive but the largest element of the cost is for labour which increases every year with inflation. The price of a hand-made welted pair of shoes was approximately £30 in 1973 making it about double that of a comparable factory-made product. The main advantage is that it will fit comfortably, a very important consideration if the feet are not a stock size.

It is quite surprising how many people have abnormalities in their feet and are compelled to have orthopaedic shoes or boots specially made for them. This accounts for a good percentage of new work that is carried out. Lasts have to be made at a cost of about £3 a pair for each individual. Once they have been made there is not a great deal of difficulty making a shoe of an unorthodox shape and the fact that the bootmaker normally retains the last more or less ensures that the replacements will be ordered from him. In most of the specifications for medical footwear it stipulates that oak-bark tanned leather must be used for the soles. People wonder who can afford these hand-made shoes. The wealthy are able to do so and sometimes young bachelors have the money and inclination to have made-to-measure footwear. Most of the personnel in the trade are middle-aged or elderly. As with so many other crafts the young are not attracted by the type of work and few apprentices are to be seen particularly if easier and better-paid factory work is available locally.

There are a large number of cobblers about doing repair work which is performed with a varying degree of skill ranging from very good to poor. Unhappily many modern factory-made shoes, particularly the ladies' fashion kind, cannot be repaired so have to be thrown away after a short amount of wear to the advantage of the manufacturers as new ones have to be bought continually.

(Opposite) Hand sewing the welt of a boot on to the upper

Leather substitutes have been tried for shoe uppers but in nearly every case the results have been unsuccessful as they do not have the breathing properties of leather. Soles are frequently of rubber or other artificial materials most of which are not particularly good for the feet and some wearers are even allergic to these types of sole.

Shoemaking is a craft that must be made to survive possibly by introducing a government subsidy for apprentices. The work is satisfying and creative and the men who do it are still old-fashioned enough to take a pride in their handicraft.

CRICKET BALLS

For over a century the best cricket balls have been made individually by the same processes. These have so far defied any mechanisation though in the cheaper balls a little machine stitching is used.

A ball is made in a distinct number of stages with craftsmen as a rule specialising in one particular operation though it is preferable for them to be able to do a second process as it helps the flexibility of the workshop.

Some balls are made in Australia, Pakistan and India but the vast majority used by counties, clubs and in matches are produced in England in the Tonbridge and Maidstone area of Kent where well over 100,000 leather balls are turned out annually.

The first job is making the centre of the ball and is called quilting. A cube of cork with sides measuring $1\frac{1}{2}$ inches is used for the centre. Corners are trimmed with a knife and worsted thread is wound round it very tightly. The worsted is worked wet in which state it becomes elastic. On drying it contracts making the ball hard and giving the quality that makes it bounce. At intervals layers of cork are introduced and the protruding pieces trimmed off. Such is the skill of the craftsmen that an astonishing degree of roundness is obtained helped by occasionally hammering the core in a hemispherical metal cup. The completed core is tested for weight then left to dry, the making of it having taken twenty minutes.

In another department the leather is prepared. The best balls are made from butts of leather, whilst the slightly thinner sides are used for the less expensive ones. Strips of white leather some 6 inches wide and 4 feet long are dyed in vats for a week and then dried. They are planed to an even thickness and cut into small pieces about 3 inches square ready for making into covers. Four pieces go to make a covering of a top-quality ball, each segment being cut using a template with a slightly bevelled edge to give a good final fit. Two segments are joined together to make a half cover. Hemp thread is used and sewn with the segments turned inside out with the stitching showing on the inside, passing through the leather but not penetrating outside it. Stitch holes are made with an awl and the thread drawn through by a length of nylon, a material that has replaced needles and pig bristle.

After stitching the half cover is turned so the proper side is on the outside and leather quarters are glued to the inside of the segments to give an even thickness. Then it is blocked out in a hydraulic press to form a perfect cup.

Next, two half covers are placed round the core and screwed up in a clamp whose jaws are two semi-circular cups that leave the join exposed. This is stitched up with one row of a specified number of stitches, the best balls having more than the cheaper kind. The stitches are made with every pair forming a knot so that if one gets broken the thread will not run back.

After being pressed for roundness the ball is ready for the final stitching of two more rows of linen thread, making in all three rows each side of the join. This is the longest operation taking about one hour. On completion the ball is ready for finishing.

The maker's name and other particulars such as 'Special County' or 'Club' are pressed on in gold leaf after which the ball is polished and varnished. It is then gauged for the correct dimension and weight and given the final inspection. Occasionally there is a reject but the percentage is extremely small.

Finally the balls are again pressed with a pressure of 5 tons to ensure perfect roundness after which they are ready for use.

At each stage there are a number of technicalities such as the waxing of threads and the preparation for softening of the leather but basically all manufacturers use the same methods about which there is no secrecy.

Good light is necessary and the temperature is kept constant to give even results.

A top-quality ball takes approximately $2\frac{1}{2}$ hours to make. It contains 2 ounces of leather out of the original 5 ounces which means that there is an unavoidable wastage of 3 ounces. It now sells at around £6, three-quarters of the cost being for labour.

It usually takes about two years for craftsmen to become fully proficient. Almost all of them are male though women do the lighter finishing jobs. Demand is constant and steady, making it difficult to build up stocks so there is no slack season and often a certain amount of overtime.

With Test Matches being televised a certain amount of attention has been given to balls supposedly losing their shape and bowlers seem to be complaining more frequently. Whilst some of their objections may be valid, a possible explanation is the fact that for some inexplicable reason some balls swing or swerve more than others. Should a bowler be unable to swing the ball to his liking he is more liable to want a replacement ball on the slightest pretext— it is part of the modern-day gamesmanship.

FALCONRY FURNITURE

Falconry has been a traditional leisure pursuit for royalty and the nobility for a very long time in this country. On the Bayeux tapestry King Harold is to be seen embarking on a visit to Normandy with a falcon perched on his arm indicating that his mission was a peaceful one.

Falconer to the King was a coveted post that existed for many years and the birds were kept in the Royal Mews. The equipment, correctly called furniture, consists of a glove for the falconer and for the bird a hood, leash, swivel, lure and bell.

The hobby of falconry is a minority one, but widespread throughout the world and every enthusiast needs a set of furniture. A few make their own while one or two professionals specialise in it.

The hoods can be most attractive and are made out of leather of any kind and colour such as cowhide, lizard or suede surmounted by a plume traditionally of herons' feathers. But as herons are now protected birds, alternatives have to be found, such as gamecocks and widgeon. The hood is an essential piece of equipment to quieten a very nervous and highly strung bird which if it could see all around would become frightened and unsettled. A falcon has bells attached to its feet so the owner can detect its presence after a flight and recover the bird.

There are a number of different types of hood, the most usual being Dutch, Indian and Arabian which differ in detail and the

A hooded peregrine falcon

Cutting leather pieces for hoods. A completed one is on the left

enthusiast chooses the one he fancies. Some have no braces, others are made on one piece and a third kind has side panels which can be made of a different sort of leather. They vary in their ornateness with the working ones being less colourful and normally having two thongs instead of plumes to facilitate the removal of the hood.

To make a hood the chosen material is cut to a pattern of the required size and shape. It is hand stitched together and wet-moulded over a wooden block to achieve the proper shape. Finally the plume or thongs are added.

The completed hood has an opening for the bird's beak and two pairs of leather thongs threaded round at neck level. By pulling one pair the hood is tightened round the bird's neck sufficiently to pre-vent it slipping off and by pulling the other pair the hood is loosened and easily removed. The price of a hood is usually £2 or £3.

An essential piece of equipment is the glove, only one is needed and normally worn on the left hand. It has to be of strong material to prevent the talons penetrating the leather which is usually of buckskin from a red deer or reindeer. The leather part has to extend right up the forearm as a falcon is not always obliging enough to perch where it is meant to on the forefinger and thumb.

CHAPTER 13

MISCELLANEOUS

CLAY PIPES

THE MAKING of pipes dates back to Elizabethan times when many of the early ones were of silver, with clay pipes soon overtaking them in numbers and popularity. In the beginning tobacco was very expensive and only the rich could afford it. Supplies were first imported from the American continent and shortly afterwards the plant began to be cultivated in this country making tobacco cheaper and more abundant. An increased number of pipes were needed and they tended to be made at first in potteries where clay and kilns were available.

Later clay-pipe making become a separate craft with over 3,000 separate manufacturers at one time.

A heavy tax was put on tobacco in the reign of James I to try and stamp it out but in spite of this the habit persisted and the monarch had to console himself with the revenue it brought in.

The earliest pipes were very small owing to the high price of tobacco. Over the years the size increased progressively and the length of the stem and ornamentation of the bowl became more ambitious. Most clay pipes are marked with the maker's initials and by their shape and markings they can usually be dated.

Manufacturers sprang up all over the country where there was suitable pipe clay, a kaolin of the china-clay type.

The pipes were made in a two-piece mould, the earliest ones being of wood, and replaced by steel at a later date.

The stem is made by rolling wet clay round a steel wire whilst the bowl is formed of a pug of moist clay which is opened out by a conical-shaped plunger. The bowl and stem are joined together by some slip, consisting of clay in solution form, then placed in the mould and when removed some hand-scraping is necessary to give a good finish. The pipe is then put in the kiln for firing in a temperature kept comparatively low to give a soft porous-finished product. A hand moulder is capable of making 500 pipes a day. The early ones had stems of 3 or 4 inches which in time became longer and the most popular pipe, the cutty, had a stem of about 7 inches and could be carried in the pocket. The longer stemmed pipes were called churchwardens and had a length of over 13 inches with some as long as a yard.

Clay pipes remained dominant for over 200 years until the coming of the cigarette at the time of the Crimean war and shortly afterwards by the briar pipe which more or less ousted the clay. The clay-pipe manufacturers mostly went out of business though a few have managed to survive and demand is once again on the increase. Those that remain are doing good business, though clay pipes are no longer made at Broseley in Shropshire which was the most important centre for their manufacture.

One of the larger manufacturers turns out several thousand a week in a variety of shapes and sizes from a large number of moulds. Clay pipes break easily but with care they last a very long time. They give a cool smoke as much of the heat is dissipated from the bowl which is hot to hold. The correct method of holding a pipe is by the stem with two fingers on top and the thumb underneath. The mouthpieces are invariably glazed usually red or green. An unglazed stem sticks to the lips, a disadvantage that was overcome in the past by dipping the end in beer. Customers used to leave their pipes in the public houses in racks provided or alternatively a pipe full of tobacco could be bought. The long churchwardens, however, were pipes that were smoked in the home, being too cumbersome to carry around.

An old pipe gives a sweeter smoke than a new one which may have traces of oil and grease that were used in the manufacture. When a pipe becomes old and stained with nicotine it can be burnt out in a fire and will emerge clean, white and like new.

With briar becoming more expensive and supplies getting scarcer there are signs that clay pipes may come into their own once more and become fashionable again.

CORN DOLLIES

Corn dollies are the name given to ornaments made of straw usually by some form of plaiting or tying. They have been made for many hundreds or even thousands of years and played their part in pagan festivities in keeping the spirit of the corn alive throughout the winter and ensuring the fertility of the soil. The making of them began to die out earlier in this century but in recent years there has been a revival of interest particularly by such organisations as the Women's Institute and they are being made again in quite large numbers and frequently with great skill.

Any straw or even grass can be used and samples can be seen using rye, barley or wheat with the latter predominating. Unfortunately there is a good deal of difficulty obtaining really suitable materials. Hardly any of the modern commercially grown wheat has the necessary characteristics. The requirement is for a good length between the wheat ear and the top joint which is the only part used. The straw has to be hollow which invariably means a winter-sown variety and nowadays most of these as well as all the spring types have a pith which renders them either unworkable or very difficult to use. Moreover chemical fertilisers and in particular nitrogen make the stems brittle and bad for dolly making. The straw must not have been harvested by a combine or any method which damages the stalk or removes the seeds.

This means that a special variety of winter wheat should be grown and then reaped using a sickle. It is best reaped when there is still some green in the stalk and in any case before birds begin to eat the seed and damage the wheat ears. It is therefore preferable to grow one's own material though with the increase in popularity and demand for suitable wheat straw a few farmers have started to grow a crop specifically for dolly making.

The straw is cut just above the top joint and the loose, covering sheath removed leaving a clean stem with a full ear of wheat which is a requirement for some patterns. If the ear is imperfect it can be cut off leaving a hollow tube of straw tapering slightly towards the top and about a foot in length. The straw dries into a golden colour with the hue varying with the year and the amount of sunshine.

The straw must be pliable and is therefore tempered by damping. This can be done by soaking for a few minutes or by holding it under a tap, care being taken not to wet it overmuch as this makes it too soft and unworkable. After wetting it can be rolled in a damp cloth ready for use. Should it dry too much it can be resoaked though if left in a damp condition it will go mildewy or black and become quite useless.

If it has to be stored for the winter beware of mice which will eat the corn even in the dolly and spoil its looks.

Most of the patterns are of very ancient origin such as the one of a female variously called Mother Earth, Harvest Queen, Ceres or Demeter.

The traditional dolly is cigar-shaped in the form of a spiral with full ears of wheat at one end. To make one of these, first a core— fat in the middle with tapering ends—is formed consisting of straw held together with raffia or cotton. Around this core the straw is woven to create the final pattern. For a simple dolly five straws are used but the number can be increased up to ten for more

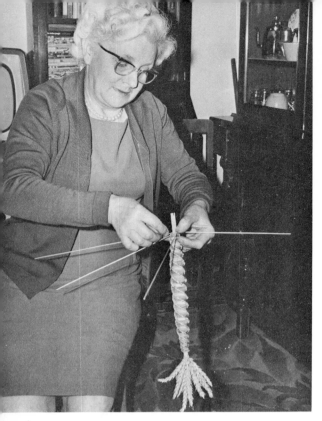

intricate and ambitious designs. When work starts each plait re-requires two movements first to bend the straw upwards and then either down or across. Failure to do this correctly may break the straw necessitating a new piece being added by sliding the thick end of a new straw over the broken piece in such a way that it will be out of sight in the finished article. When making a dolly it has to be held well away from the body to avoid injuring the straws which stick out from the work. A good dolly looks neat, with the straw carefully selected to be of uniform thickness. The work requires patience and persistence because once started it has to be continued till the article is finished or the straw will dry out and become unmanageable. A stint of up to three or four hours may be needed for an advanced pattern. A major fault amongst beginners is to squeeze the straw flat and pull it too hard spoiling the work.

A finished corn dolly. They will last for fifty years or longer

A degree of proficiency can be achieved quite quickly by some whilst others never can master the art.

Some dollies are plaited on a curve, for instance in the case of a horseshoe. In such cases the core can be formed round a piece of short wire bent to the required shape.

The craft has become popular in recent years as dollies are in demand for decoration and it is a craft that women like and do well whilst some artists make them professionally for the tourist trade. Some are excellently made but it will be a pity if the market becomes flooded with too many commercial products.

Straw dollies keep a long time—possibly up to fifty years or longer if kept in a case. Should they become dusty they can be washed clean.

177

CIDER MAKING

The Romans made cider and its production has continued ever since then though is now confined exclusively to the Worcester, Somerset and West Country areas.

The true rural cider, sometimes referred to as rough cider or scrumpy, consists entirely of fermented apple juice which is free from additives, whereas the factory-made drink is made under carefully controlled conditions to give a standard product year after year.

The manufacturer carries out the following sequence:

1   Adds sulphites to suppress the wild yeasts.
2   Adds yeast to ferment the apple juice.
3   Adds sugar and water.
4   Adds colouring matter.

Apples are specially grown for cider making and are carefully sprayed and fertilised to give the best results under increasingly scientific conditions.

Harvesting of the apples takes place in the autumn. The producers do not pick them but wait till they fall to the ground then collect them into sacks. Those that have rotted brown still make perfectly good cider but black rot does not. By this time they are ripe and the cider making continues until Christmas. As a cottage industry it still continues on a significant scale. The first operation is to reduce the apple to pulp which used to be done by rolling it with a runner stone placed on end and hauled round a circular trough by a horse squashing the apples to pomace. Today this is usually done with an electric motor which performs the job more quickly and efficiently.

The pomace is next spread out on a cloth that was once of hair, then hessian and now usually nylon, till an area of about a square yard is covered to a depth of 2 or 3 inches. The cloth is then folded over to make a cheese. Some countrymen strongly advocate the use of straw between the layers of pomace while another school of thought maintains this is unnecessary and might give the cider a fusty taste if the straw has been badly stored.

When about twenty cheeses have been prepared, they are placed under a press and the pomace squashed, the liquid then being taken to wooden barrels for fermenting. The barrels are usually old wine or spirit ones made of oak or chestnut. Very soon the apple juice begins a violent ferment lasting several days during which most impurities come to the top and flow out of the bung hole of the barrel. The ferment slowly simmers down but continues for several weeks. During this time the barrel must be kept topped up with no air in the top or there will be a danger of the contents turning to vinegar. Incidentally apple vinegar is very good though not the product the cider maker wants. The bung hole is plugged by a rag during fermentation on completion of which a wooden one replaces it.

A mobile cider-making machine. Apples are put into the hopper on the right and minced to a pomace. This is then transferred from the trough to the press and the liquid pours out into the bucket on the left

After a month or two the cider is ready for drinking, though it goes on improving and maturing for some months.

There is a good steady demand for scrumpy. It is sold in some public houses whilst many regular customers come along with their containers to buy it straight from the barrel at about 40p a gallon.

The alcoholic content and degree of sweetness of cottage cider varies with the type of apple and the growing conditions. Cider can be made out of any apples though the special varieties with a sharp taste give the best drink. It is likely to be about twice as alcoholic as beer as well as being half the price and it is very inadvisable to drink more than two pints.

One ton of apples convert into 15 hundredweight of cider, the pressed apple pulp being fed to cows. There is a certain amount of wastage in the form of sludge in the bottom of each barrel which can be given to pigs.

For cottage-cider making on a lesser scale there are the mobile cider machines which used to be hauled round to the village orchards in turn. At one end is a hopper into which the apples are poured and ground into pomace by two grinding wheels operated by a hand-wheel. The pomace falls into a large trough whence it is scooped up and made into a cheese which is then squeezed by screwing down a hand-press.

DEW PONDS

The making of dew ponds is more or less a dead craft, the last one I know of being made in 1940 by men who are still alive today. Though they may no longer be made, the principles of their construction are still needed to make ornamental ponds and repair canal beds.

Their original use was to provide watering-places on the downs or uplands for the thousands of sheep that were pastured on them.

If properly maintained a dew pond can last almost indefinitely but lack of maintenance and hooves of cattle quite quickly destroy the clay puddle causing the water to escape. Some are supposedly of great antiquity though evidence of their age is hard to come by as they may have been rebuilt or reconstructed.

The name dew pond is something of a misnomer and was first used in Victorian times. Dew may have helped a little to keep up the water-level though it probably only compensated for the natural evaporation. They were built mostly on the sides of a hill in a natural depression and filled almost entirely by rainwater. It is extremely rare to find one right on the crest of a hill.

They were mainly constructed in chalky country and the vital requirement was for them to be watertight.

They were made in the following manner. First an area of 20 or 30 square yards was dug out to give a depth of between 6 and 10 feet in the middle. If a natural depression could be found this minimised the work. Alternatively by digging in to a slight slope the displaced earth could be made to form a retaining wall which

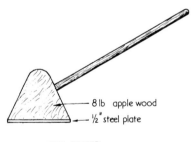

— 8 lb apple wood
— ½" steel plate

THE BEATER

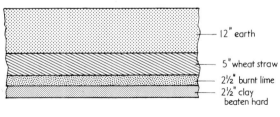

— 12" earth

— 5" wheat straw
— 2½" burnt lime
— 2½" clay
  beaten hard

SECTION THROUGH POND

Making a dew pond

181

had to be consolidated. Having excavated a basin of the required dimensions, sometimes with the help of gelignite, it had to be lined with puddled clay to make it watertight. A quantity of clay about 5 inches in depth was spread over the depression, usually provided by the farmer who wanted the pond, and this was consolidated into an impervious layer of about $2\frac{1}{2}$ inches by means of beating with a wooden mallet or beetle, weighing about 8 pounds, with a steel sole. Clay in a field is porous, but if puddled and kneaded with water it becomes watertight.

The clay bed of a dew pond was the most important feature and the expenditure of hard labour in beating it solid accounted for most of the work. Care had to be taken that at this stage the clay did not crack either by becoming frozen in winter, when work had to stop, or drying out in summer. The latter could be avoided by placing moist straw over the uncompleted work. Having beaten the clay to a glassy smooth surface it was covered with a 2-inch layer of lime which set the clay brick hard making it impenetrable by worms. The practice of the Wiltshire pond makers was to put a layer of straw over the clay, a feature not normally to be found elsewhere. Over this was put the steaning consisting of a 1-foot layer of earth to protect the clay. Sometimes hard core was added to give additional protection particularly if cattle were to drink from the pond.

Most of the ponds were wired off so that livestock would not wander about all over them possibly causing damage.

The later ponds often had land drains leading down to keep them filled up and also a drinking trough below supplied by a syphon so the pond itself did not become trodden. The water in dew ponds was crystal clear, the shepherds assisting by removing any weeds.

Maintenance was required to stop them silting up and to prevent rushes and trees growing their roots into the clay puddle and puncturing it. Trees were acceptable nearby to give shade. With the virtual disappearance of the downland flocks of sheep, the ponds are no longer needed and nearly all have become neglected. The puddles become cracked, water leaks out and they form an unwanted

An old dew pond that is becoming overgrown and will soon disappear

depression in the ground that can be ploughed through with comparative ease—the fate of the majority.

A good number are still to be seen though they are slowly deteriorating and will have soon vanished from the scene.

FLINT KNAPPING

The splitting of flints is called knapping and the craft has been practised in a variety of ways for thousands of years. Primitive man became highly skilled in making from flints such items as axes, arrow heads and scrapers. Flint is one of the purest forms of silica and is commonly found in chalk where there are seams of it. Another place to find it is on the seashores by chalk cliffs where they become washed and smoothed by the movement of the sea. A flint in time develops a white outer surface but when split the inside is very dark. Grimes Graves in Norfolk give an indication of the importance of flint where over 300 pits covering 35 acres were dug chiefly in the Stone Age.

Flints were used for some buildings when supplies were at hand locally and where stone was not so readily available. Sometimes they were used whole but in the thirteenth century they began to be knapped and a century later were sometimes squared as well. The knapping is done by striking the flint in a particular way and exploiting any lines of weakness. It is skilled work but the expert can achieve a very high degree of proficiency which is shown when the flints are squared to a dimension of about 4 inches. This is a laborious and expensive operation and confined to important positions of churches such as gateways. The flints are always used in conjunction with other materials, mostly brick or stone. In building a peak was reached in 'flushwork' in which knapped flints form a pattern with the stonework. Building in flint was practised more extensively in East Anglia than elsewhere but it is to be found over a wide area though its aesthetic appeal is not very great and brick and stone are usually preferred. The result is that knapping has virtually disappeared and when recently some knapped flints were needed for part of the building of the University of Sussex it had to be done by a Belgian craftsman.

However, the most important use of flint was for firearms where the wheel-lock gun succeeded the old matchlock and the priming powder was ignited by sparks given off by a wheel revolving on a flint in the manner of the present-day cigarette lighter. This was superseded by the flintlock around the time of the Civil War and this weapon is still in use today in many less advanced countries. The flint required is approximately an inch square and is held in a piece of leather which in turn is held in a pair of steel jaws and clamped up tight.

To fire a flintlock the following sequence is carried out in a muzzle loader:

1 The charge consisting of powder and a ball is rammed down the muzzle and kept in place by a wad.
2 The weapon is primed by placing a small amount of powder in the priming-pan after which it is closed by the cover to which is attached the steel.
3 The striking hammer which holds the flint is drawn back to full cock.

4   The trigger is pressed. The hammer springs forward, the flint strikes the serrated face of the steel at the same time forcing it out of the way which uncovers the priming powder. A spark is made and the primer is ignited and finally this fires the charge.

The flintlock reigned supreme for almost 200 years until the coming of the percussion cap around 1830. There are many hundreds of flintlocks in India, Africa and America that are still used today. Moreover as a hobby flintlock gun shooting is becoming very popular particularly in America so the demand for hints is still very large. In this country the knapping of gun flints has been done almost exclusively at Brandon in Norfolk, where the industry reached its zenith during the Napoleonic Wars when there were 200 knappers at work turning out 356,000 flints a month to meet the requirements of the army. Now only Mr Edwards of Brandon is left making them professionally.

There is no secret about knapping. The process is straightforward, but a lot of skill and knowledge is needed to attain a reasonable output. The production of gun flints requires three distinct operations: first squaring the flint; then flaking; and finally knapping. The process of making them is as follows:

Squaring   The flint is put on a pad on the left knee and struck in exactly the right place with a 4 pound hammer to obtain a square of about 6 inches.

Flaking   The square is put on the left leg and flakes are knocked off. These are about 4 inches long and 1 inch wide and naturally come off with a bevelled edge. A craftsman can knock off several hundred flakes an hour.

Knapping   A wooden block is used into which is fixed a piece of metal with a sloping edge. The flake is placed on this and hit with a hammer made out of an old file. The flake is broken off with various sizes but the majority are about 1 inch square.

Soldiers or sportsmen kept a supply of flints in a small bag as replacements were often needed, there being a limit to the number of times they could be used once bits had flaked off.

HORN WORK

Horn has been used in a number of ways for many centuries. Items made from it that readily come to mind are drinking-cups, powder-flasks, shoe-horns, combs, snuff-boxes, spoons, hearing-trumpets, etc.

Cow horn was always plentiful and in certain districts there was deer antler as well. The fashioning of it never became a great industry, but local people were able to make articles out of it to meet the demand. Up till 200 years ago the predominant breed of cattle was longhorns and as their name implies they had an excellent spread of horn.

Longhorns were superseded by shorthorns which in spite of their name had horns of a reasonable size. As a generalisation only cow horns were used and these are hollow till near the tip. Horn is easily cut with a saw and when heated becomes pliable enabling it to be pressed out quite thin and flat. The heat has to be sufficient for it to remain in its new form without springing back to the original shape, but not too great or it will burn.

Up till Elizabethan times when only the Church and the very rich were able to afford glass for windows, horn was sometimes used in its place to let a little light filter through into the house. To this day many old craftsmen use a horn as a receptacle to hold their grease or tallow.

Other properties are the fact that it can be polished to a very high degree and materials do not readily adhere to it so it is often employed by potters and used for egg spoons.

Practically all the horn work in England today is carried out at the Abbey Horn Works in Kendal which employs around a dozen craftsmen.

Unfortunately far less native cow horn is available now due to the almost universal practice of dehorning cattle and nearly all of it has to be imported from Africa.

The horn from some types of ram and deer antlers are solid and apart from not being so universally available are not used as much. They are, however, very suitable for such items as handles of walking-sticks and knives, the manufacture of which mostly takes place in Scotland where supplies are more abundant.

HORSEHAIR FOR INDUSTRY

For many years horsehair has been used for a variety of purposes and there were at one time a number of firms that bought and processed it when there was a large, native, horse population. Over the years the number has dwindled to one small but important firm, that of Arnold & Gould of Glemsford in Suffolk who handle approximately 100 tons of the commodity every year. Supplies come mainly from abroad including China, Russia, Mongolia and the Argentine, whilst in Britain it comes from the slaughterers' yards.

Of the tonnage used about 75 per cent is from the tails and the rest from the manes, the former being called stiff and the latter soft.

Horsehair grows at the rate of about $1\frac{1}{2}$ pounds a year in the tail (with a long and large one weighing 3 pounds) and 1 pound a year for the mane.

In this country horsehair may be cut but docking which is the actual cutting of the fleshy end of the tail has been forbidden by law for the last sixteen years.

The colour of hair ranges from black, grey, brown to white. The latter is the most valuable and accounts for 8 per cent of the total supply. Some of the blond hair is bleached white and white hair can be dyed any colour.

The hair has to pass through twenty separate processes before it is finally ready for despatch.

It usually arrives in large bales weighing anything up to 500 pounds. First it has to be disinfected. Next it is hand-sorted into half a dozen different grades of tails, manes, colours and lengths. Following this it is washed in soft water, then wet hackled. This consists of pulling the hair through steel combs secured to the bench and pointing vertically upwards, which removes the short hairs and gets the remainder lying in the same direction. The hair is then dried on wooden racks before being bundled and double-drawn by women through similar steel combs to those used in wet hackling. This action is repeated after which the hair is bunched by hand into small locks of even lengths. The top of the bunch is patted level with a wooden bat that beats down protruding hairs. The bunches are then tied and the ends guillotined to give a very neat finish with a diameter of about $1\frac{1}{2}$ inches and a length varying from an inch or two to 34 inches or more. Finally it is sent to the packing department where the bundles are sorted into their different lengths and colours ready for despatch.

Approximately a quarter of the production is exported, English-dressed hair enjoying a good reputation for quality. The rest goes to the home market.

One of the main uses for the hair is for brushes both for domestic needs and also in all shapes and sizes for industrial use, particularly where price does not matter as it costs about twice to three times as much as nylon.

Under a microscope it can be seen that the hair has an outer covering of scales rather similar to a fish and in using a brush it is the sides of the hair and not the ends that do most of the sweeping and give it efficiency. The particular construction of the hair makes it indispensable for violin bows as it is the only hair of the required length (about 30 inches) available in quantity.

Some is mixed with hog bristle for paint brushes in which case the ends are flagged (frayed) in order to help retain the paint.

Other uses include textile furnishing where it provides the weft and in inner linings for lapels of suits since the hair has good resilience always springing back to shape—a feature that it retains for years.

Wigs for judges and barristers are made from it, no less than 8 hundredweight a year being needed for this purpose; also military plumes and fly-whisks.

Shorter lengths are sent to be curled for use in some of the best-quality mattresses and upholstery, so virtually no hair is wasted. Horsehair is unharmed by most chemicals and acids and recovers from wetting.

Nothing has been devised to mechanise any part of the processing which relies on the skill and dexterity of the craft's men and women employees.

There has been a significant revival in demand for horsehair recently which seems to be a common experience in many crafts as shortcomings reveal themselves in many of the synthetic substitutes.

RIDING-WHIPS

With the enormous international increase in the horse population, almost all of it for leisure, a heavy burden has been put on the suppliers of equipment, none more so than on the makers of whips.

The biggest maker of them is the old-established firm of Swaine, Adeney & Brigg, founded in 1750, who enjoy a world-wide reputation for the quality and variety of their article and who produce 4,000 whips a month.

They list no less than 150 different kinds and in addition can always make one specially to order. The price can vary from £2 or £3 for a simple one to a three figure sum for a luxury type with gold bands.

They have to be made individually and there is little scope for mechanisation resulting in everything having to be hand-made which requires a good deal of skill. Specialised whips are required for hunting, beagling, dogs, racing, dressage, polo, riding and driving.

The majority of whips have a core that may be of nylon, steel, rawhide or fibreglass. Some difficulty was experienced initially with the former as it had to have the correct whippiness and flexibility but this problem has now been satisfactorily resolved. In the past whalebone was used extensively, but supplies have diminished drastically.

The cores are covered by such materials as linen or nylon braid, leather plaiting or stitched leather. The braid is plaited on by a special machine, being one of the few processes that can be mechanised.

Plaiting and stitching is all hand-done, sometimes by women working in their homes. After the covering has been put on the whip it is rolled under pressure to make the finish perfectly smooth.

There are a large variety of different keepers ranging from plaited thongs to small stitched keepers used by jockeys. Similarly there are a wide range of finishes for the handles. These may be of stag horn, leather, ivory or metal caps stuck on by whipmakers' pitch consisting of a mixture of resin and glue.

Whips for driving horse-drawn vehicles are a speciality on their own. They are mostly made from holly and the shaft has to be perfectly straight and about 6 feet in length which presents a problem obtaining the material. First the bark is removed and then the shaft is left to season for eighteen months after which it is rubbed down with sandpaper though the small protrusions are usually left. The whip has to feel right with the correct balance and the desired amount of flexibility. This can be achieved by sandpapering till the required result is obtained after which it is given a coat of varnish.

It then has the handle fitted, consisting of a mild drawn-steel tube which in turn has a cap put on the end which can be of gold, silver or any chosen metal. The handle is usually covered in hand-stitched hogskin or morocco leather with a metal collar at the top.

The other end of the whip has to have a slight swan neck. This is cleverly obtained by cutting a pair of 12-inch long goose feathers to give a quilled finish by securing one each side of the top of the whip. The whip is then fitted with a white leather plaited thong made from sheepskin or goatskin which is bound to the whip over the quills with linen-tent thread finished in an attractive pattern and making the completed article a work of art.

ROPE MAKING

The making of rope by hand is uneconomical and has ceased on a commercial scale. The man who claims to be the last full-time hand-maker is the famous Herbert Marrison who works in the centuries-old rope walk in the Peak Cavern at Castleton in Derbyshire. He is eighty-nine years of age and is on the point of retirement. In addition possibly a few others follow the craft on a part-time basis.

It can be made out of a wide variety of materials that include hemp, jute, sisal, manilla, flax, cotton, and modern man-made fibres such as nylon.

The yarn is nowadays bought ready-made as the spinning of it by hand is slow and uneconomical.

To make rope the first process is warping in which the yarn is attached to a hook on a jack, or strand twister. The rope maker walks down the rope walk paying out the yarn keeping it off the ground by laying it over the top of T-pieces about 3 feet in height and placed at intervals of about 12 yards, the number depending on the length of the rope being made, which can be 100 yards or more. In making up the rope it loses about a quarter of the length of the warp so allowance has to be made for this.

The rope maker walks up and down with his warp until there is enough to make a strand. The far ends are secured to a horse or traveller. This may be on wheels or simply a heavy weight that is dragged along the ground to give tension to the rope as it is twisted up, the tension being varied as necessary by altering the weight of the traveller. For a three-stranded rope the process is repeated three times. Each strand is attached to a separate hook on the strand twister but all three are secured to a single hook on the horse. In warping, the rope maker may walk many miles a day when making a long length.

The 200-year-old rope walk in the Peak Cavern, Castleton, Derbyshire. Warping is in progress

After warping is complete the strands are twisted by turning a crank handle on the jack, the rope maker using his experience to know how much twisting is needed. When this point has been reached a top is inserted between the strands at the far end by the horse. The top is a piece of hardwood such as box or beech with three grooves, one for each strand.

The twisting continues, this usually being the job for a lad, and the rope maker slowly walks along holding the top and the three strands form up into a length of rope behind it. The speed at which the craftsman moves regulates the hardness of the rope and is judged by experience. As work proceeds the horse is dragged forward slowly due to the rope being shortened by the twisting. When the whole rope has been made up into a single piece with three strands the ends are secured to one hook and a back twist is

(Opposite) Mr Marrison, the last professional rope maker, walking along with his top. The rope is taking shape behind him

put in the rope. This makes it tight and prevents kinking. Most rope is a little untidy at this stage so that it may be dressed with flour paste mixed with size. This is rubbed on with a rag and gives it a tidy finish.

The rope is then unhooked and the ends are either whipped, spliced or knotted to stop them from fraying and unwinding.

Though the craftsmen have vanished, rope walks still exist all over the country. They were mainly out of doors, often under trees to give some shelter, and many were of a length of several hundred yards. A good example is at Bridport in Dorsetshire where the pavements are exceptionally wide to give room for the walk.

CANE SEATS

Cane has been used for the seats and backs of furniture since its introduction from Holland about 250 years ago. Its popularity declined with the advent of padded upholstery and is not now used much for new furniture though there are plenty of antiques that need to be kept in repair.

Chair cane comes from rattan which grows in the East Indies as a long rambling climber. It comes from the outside bark which is first split into a number of segments that are then passed through cutting blades, one set to plane the strand to a uniform thickness and the other to give an even width. The outside of the cane is shiny and pale in colour becoming darker with age. The strands can be as long as 12 yards and are sold by weight in a number of different grades or thicknesses, a heavier grade being used for seats and a slightly finer one for the backs of chairs though the permutations of these can be varied.

Work is progressed by interlacing the cane which forms a pattern as it is threaded through the holes around the perimeter of the article being worked. A fair degree of proficiency can be reached in a few weeks though there are a number of snags and difficulties to be overcome. The shiny side has to be uppermost, joints must be hidden underneath, there must be no kinking nor any mistakes.

Difficulties begin at once as practically nothing is square so that skill is required to avoid the finished pattern being on the skew. All chairs are different, even those in a supposedly matching set.

The tension has to be the same throughout, a difficulty being that the pattern tightens as the work progresses and more strands are interwoven. At all stages care is necessary to avoid cutting the hands on the cane.

The work cannot be hurried so that an average chair with a seat and back might take 18 hours to recane using about $\frac{1}{2}$ pound of material. This means that labour accounts for about 90 per cent of the cost of repair.

Before starting work the cane has to be soaked for a few minutes to make it more pliable. The old cane has to be cut out and the holes, many of which have wooden pegs in them, have to be cleaned out. There are a number of different patterns that can be used, the most frequent being the seven-step pattern.

A cane seat and back with the repair work at different stages of progress and the craftsmen's tools displayed

The stages are: singling, doubling, setting, crossing, crossing in the opposite direction, pegging and beading.

It is normal in the first stage to commence at the centre and work outwards in threading the strands from the back to the front of the seat. In stage two this is repeated to give a double set of strands using the same holes.

Stage three is setting, in which two strands are passed through holes and worked at right angles to those in the first two stages, one being threaded over and under and the other under and over to produce an interlocking mesh.

In stages four and five the strands are interwoven diagonally, one set from right to left and the other at right angles.

Stage six consists of driving wooden pegs into alternate holes to hold the pattern and finally the beading is put around and fixed in position by loops of cane in alternate holes.

In all stages the cane is held tight either by inserting wooden pegs in the holes or by pushing in a doubler, similar to a bodkin, to hold the strand.

The tools required are few and of a simple design so are comparatively cheap. They consist of a knife, hammer, wooden pegs, awl, bodkin, doubler and a shell bodkin. The initial outlay is therefore not expensive, little extra room is needed as a working-space and mess is made only from pieces of cane that have been cut.

There will always be a demand for craftsmen who can repair the large number of cane seats still in use and it is a craft that can be done very adequately by the blind.

RUSH SEATS

Rush seating is comparatively cheap and the method of weaving can soon be learnt with work proceeding quickly.

The rush used is *Scirpus lacustris* which grows near streams in most parts of the country. It is possible to collect it around July but care has to be taken in drying it. If done too slowly, mould might attack it, and if too quickly, brittleness will result.

For use it has to be made pliable by damping to a degree that has to be gauged by experience.

To reseat a chair the old rush is first removed. A square seat presents no problems but seats are invariably wider at the front so that care is necessary to compensate for this. A loop is made around the back of the chair and some rush secured to this.

As work proceeds the rush is continually twisted to give it strength. For fine work a single rush can be used though two or three are normal. As one piece of rush comes to an end another piece is introduced and with some experience an even thickness can be made. A difficulty to be overcome is the fact that a rush tapers towards the top so a new piece has to be let in at regular intervals.

The first rush, secured to the back of the chair, is brought forward over the bar at the front, threaded underneath and brought up over the top of the first rush and turned round the side where the process is repeated. The movements are less complicated than they sound, and by working clockwise round the outside, the characteristic pattern begins to take shape and fills up towards the centre till it is finally closed, with any ends and untidy pieces out of sight underneath.

The reseating is done with the rush in a moist condition so that when it has been completed it is essential to dry it comparatively quickly to prevent mould attacking it.

APPENDICES

I

BECOMING A CRAFTSMAN

For those who aspire to become a craftsman it is usual to serve an apprenticeship, in most cases by working with a professional. Qualifications are no longer so necessary and of more importance is a reputation acquired over the years by a mixture of diligence, skill, hard work and plenty of practical experience.

If anybody has difficulty in finding a craftsman to learn from he should approach the Council of Small Industries in Rural Areas (CoSIRA) who have regional representatives covering the whole country. CoSIRA themselves run a number of 'topping up' courses to finish off the training of apprentices in such crafts as thatching and farriery. In addition most of the numerous art schools run courses in pottery, weaving, wood-carving and wrought-iron work.

Craftsmanship is being appreciated to an increasing extent and anybody qualifying today should have an assured future providing he also has a certain amount of business acumen.

2

WHERE TO SEE CRAFTSMEN

It is possible to see country craftsmen at work and by far the best guide is published annually by the Council of Small Industries in Rural Areas, usually abbreviated to CoSIRA. The booklet is *CoSIRA Guide to Country Workshops in Britain* modestly priced at 10p and is obtainable from CoSIRA, 35 Camp Road, Wimbledon Common, London SW19 4UP. There are many more craftsmen who avoid publicity and who have to be sought out by enquiring about them in the district being visited, a good source of information usually being the local public house or village shops.

Craftsmen frequently give demonstrations at agricultural shows throughout the country with crowds always gathering around and showing a great interest in whatever work they are doing be it horse shoeing, wrought-iron work, basketry, etc.

Another good booklet is *Scottish Crafts and Craftsmen* obtainable from The Scottish Craft Centre, Acheson House, Canon-gate, Edinburgh.

3

CRAFTS MUSEUMS

These fall into two categories. First there are the conventional museums with a section devoted to crafts, in particular those of their locality, and then there are the open-air museums which are a comparatively new idea that is catching the imagination of the public. The whereabouts of these can be found in a very comprehensive booklet *Museums and Galleries in Great Britain and Ireland*. This is published annually by ABC Travel Guides Ltd, Oldhill, London Road, Dunstable LU6 3EB, and should be found in shops such as W. H. Smith & Son Ltd.

Open-air museums are steadily increasing their scope and quite large buildings are transported to the site and re-erected. Exhibits of this sort are those such as the windmill at the Avoncroft Museum and various blacksmiths' shops. A particularly good one of this type is the Welsh Folk Museum at St Fagan's Castle near Cardiff whilst other notable examples are the Weald Museum at Singleton in Hampshire, the Avoncroft Museum at Bromsgrove, the Abbot's Hall Museum at Stowmarket, the Ryedale Folk Museum at Hutton-le-Hole in Yorkshire and the Ironbridge Gorge Museum in Shropshire, to mention a few.

Of the conventional museums the Museum of English Rural Life at Reading is excellent and the York Castle Museum is outstanding. Most large towns are very well served and it would be invidious to single them out. A number of museums of crafts and bygones are also to be found in the outbuildings of some of the great houses that are open to the public.

Now that the trend is towards better presentation, they are of increasing interest to young and old alike.

BIBLIOGRAPHY

For the serious researcher there are two excellent pamphlets listing a comprehensive range of books and articles on crafts:

Crafts, Trades and Industries, a Book List for Local Historians, obtainable from the National Council of Social Service, 26 Bedford Square, London WC1 (1968)
Select List of Books and Information Sources on Trades, Crafts and Small Industries in Rural Areas, published by CoSIRA, 35 Camp Road, Wimbledon Common, London SW19 4UP (1973)

In addition the Forestry Commission publish a large number of informative booklets and leaflets on all aspects of their work. The list is obtainable from Her Majesty's Stationery Office. CoSIRA also produce several books, booklets and leaflets on crafts. The following three are comprehensive, informative and very well illustrated:

Arnold, James. *The Shell Book of Country Crafts* (John Baker, 1968)
Edlin, H. L. *Woodland Crafts in Britain* (repr David & Charles, 1973)

Jenkins, J. Geraint. *Traditional Country Craftsmen* (Routledge & Kegan Paul, 1965)

Some books on specific subjects are listed below:

The Blacksmith's Craft (CoSIRA, 1964)
Freese, Stanley. *Windmills and Millwrighting* (David & Charles, 1971)
Hasluck, P. *Saddlery and Harness Making* (W. E. Allen, 1962)
Lambeth, M. *The Golden Dolly* (John Baker, 1969)
Lister, G. B. *Decorative Wrought Ironwork in Great Britain* (David & Charles, 1970)
Reynolds, J. *Watermills and Windmills* (Evelyn, 1970)
Syson, L. *British Water Mills* (Batsford, 1965)
The Thatcher's Craft (CoSIRA, 1961)
Wailes, Rex. *The English Windmill* (Routledge & Kegan Paul, 1954)
Webber, Ronald. *The Village Blacksmith* (David & Charles, 1971)
Wright, Dorothy. *Baskets and Basketry* (David & Charles, 1972)

The 'Discovery' series of booklets published by Shire Publications, Tring, Herts, are very informative. Those dealing with crafts are continually being added to and include the following subjects: Carts and Waggons, Harness and Saddlery, Horse Brasses, Watermills, Windmills and Wrought Iron.

INDEX

Page references in bold numerals indicate illustrations